सीताराम

Rāma-Hymns

Hanumān-Chālisa
Rāma-Rakshā-Stotraṁ
Bhushumdi-Rāmayana
Nāma-Rāmayanam
Rāma-Ashtottara-Shata-Nāma-Stotra
Rāma-Ashtottara-Shata-Nāmā-Vali
Rāma-Ashtakam & other Hymns

with Devanagari Text, Transliteration & English Translation

—:—

राम-जप

श्रीहनुमान-चालीसा
श्रीरामरक्षास्तोत्र
श्रीकाकभुसुंडिरामायण
श्रीनामरामायणम
श्रीरामाष्टोत्तरशतनामस्तोत्रं
श्रीरामाष्टोत्तरशतनामावलि
श्रीरामाष्टकम् - इत्यादि

Composed by

Tulsidas
& other Ancient Sages of India

Published by: only **RAMA** only
(an Imprint of e1i1 Corporation)

Title: **Rama-Hymns**

Sub-Title: **Hanuman-Chalisa, Rama-Raksha-Stotra, Bhushumdi-Ramayana, Nama-Ramayana, Rama-Shata-Nama-Stotra, Rama-Ashtakam and other Hymns**
with Devanagari Text, Transliteration & English Translation

Authors of Devanagari Texts: **Tulsidas, and others Ancient Sages of India**
Translator: **Sushma**

Cover Design: **Sushma**

Identifiers
Library of Congress Control Number: 2018938535
ISBN: **978-1-945739-25-5** (Paperback)
ISBN: **978-1-945739-09-5** (Hardcover)

—o—

—o—

www.**e1i1**.com -- www.**OnlyRama**.com
email: **e1i1***books***e1i1**@gmail.com

— CONTENTS —

(Devanagari Text with English Translation & Transliteration)

श्रीहनुमान-आरती . śrī-hanumāna āratī – 4

श्रीहनुमान-चालीसा . śrī-hanumāna-cālīsā – 7

श्रीरामरक्षा-स्तोत्र . śrī-rāma-rakṣā-stotra – 15

श्रीकाकभुसुंडि-रामायण . śrī-kāka-bhusuṁḍi-rāmāyaṇa – 27

श्रीनाम-रामायणम . śrī-nāma-rāmāyaṇam – 35

श्रीरामाष्टोत्तर-शतनाम-स्तोत्रं . śrī-rām-āṣṭottara-śata-nāma-stotraṁ – 47

श्रीरामाष्टोत्तर-शतनामावलि . śrī-rām-āṣṭottara-śata-nāmā-valiḥ – 53

श्रीरामाष्टकम् . śrī-rāmāṣṭakam - 61

श्रीराम-स्तुति . śrī-rāma-stuti – 64

श्रीहनुमान-स्तुति . śrī-hanumāna-stuti - 66

—o—

(Devanagari Text with Transliteration)

श्रीगणेश-पञ्चरत्नस्तोत्रं . śrī-gaṇeśa-pañcaratna-stotraṁ – 68

शिवनाम-जप . śivanāma-japa – 70

श्रीरामायण-आरती . śrī rāmāyaṇa āratī – 71

जय जगदीश हरे आरती . jaya jagadīśa hare āratī – 72

श्रीहनुमान-चालीसा . śrī-hanumāna-cālīsā – 74

—o—

(Devanagari Text only)

श्रीहनुमान-चालीसा – 76

श्रीरामरक्षा-स्तोत्र – 78

श्रीकाकभुसुंडि-रामायण – 82

श्रीरामाष्टोत्तर-शतनाम-स्तोत्रं – 84

श्रीरामाष्टोत्तर-शतनामावलि – 86

श्रीरामाष्टकम् – 88

श्रीनाम-रामायणम – 89

श्रीराम-स्तुति – 92

श्रीहनुमान-स्तुति – 92

—o—

— Other Contents —

Guide to Pronunciation

About Rāmcharitmānas and Tulsīdās

श्री हनुमान आरती — śrī hanumāna āratī

आरती कीजै हनुमान लला की, दुष्ट-दलन रघुनाथ कला की.[1]
āratī kījai hanumāna lalā kī, duṣṭa-dalana raghunātha kalā kī.
जाके बल से गिरिवर काँपै, रोग दोष जाके निकट न झाँपै.[2]
jāke bala se girivara kām̐pai, roga doṣa jāke nikaṭa na jhām̐pai.
अंजनि-पुत्र महा बल दाई, संतन के प्रभु सदा सहाई.[3]
aṁjani-putra mahā bala dāī, saṁtana ke prabhu sadā sahāī.
दे बीरा रघुनाथ पठाये, लंका जारि सीय सुधि लाये.[4]
de bīrā raghunātha paṭhāye, laṁkā jāri sīya sudhi lāye.
लंका-सो कोट समुद्र-सी खाई, जात पवनसुत बार न लाई.[5]
laṁkā-so koṭa samudra-sī khāī, jāta pavanasuta bāra na lāī.
लंका जारि असुर संहारे, सियारामजी के काज सँवारे.[6]
laṁkā jāri asura saṁhāre, siyārāmajī ke kāja sam̐vāre.
लछिमन मूर्छित पड़े सकारे, आनि सजीवन प्रान उबारे.[7]
lachimana mūrchita paṛe sakāre, āni sajīvana prāna ubāre.
पैठी पताल तोरि जम-कारे, अहिरावन की भुजा उखारे.[8]
paiṭhī patāla tori jama-kāre, ahirāvana kī bhujā ukhāre.
बायें भुजा असुरदल मारे, दहिने भुजा संतजन तारे.[9]
bāyeṁ bhujā asuradala māre, dahine bhujā saṁtajana tāre.
सुर नर मुनि आरती उतारे, जै जै जै हनुमान उचारे.[10]
sura nara muni āratī utāre, jai jai jai hanumāna ucāre.
कंचन थार कपूर लौ छाई, आरति करत अंजना माई.[11]
kaṁcana thāra kapūra lau chāī, ārati karata aṁjanā māī.
जो हनुमानजी की आरति गावै, बसि बैकुंठ परमपद पावै.[12]
jo hanumānajī kī ārati gāvai, basi baikuṁṭha paramapada pāvai.

आरती कीजै हनुमान लला की, दुष्ट-दलन रघुनाथ कला की ...
āratī kījai hanumāna lalā kī, duṣṭa-dalana raghunātha kalā kī ...

Rāma-Hymns राम-जप

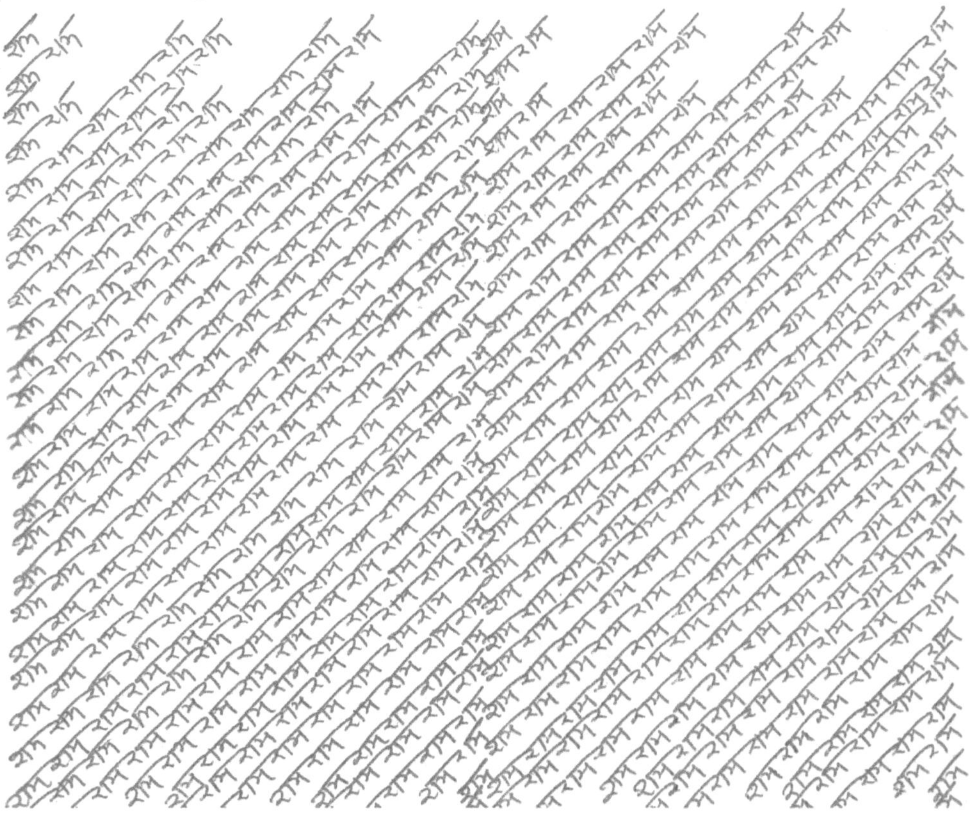

A NOTE:

In Sanskrit, when the sound changes occur at word boundaries, a fusion process sets in -- called *sandhi*. This causes adjacent words to get combined, and sometimes the resultant word becomes quite long. Naturally, this results in the Transliterated word becoming lengthy as well.

So during the process of Transliteration, we decided to add hyphens (-) at certain places (mainly Sanskrit words)—in order to improve readability for the uninitiated. Please note that these hyphen-breaks are *not* necessarily accurate—either phonetically or by word-*sandhi*—but they certainly make reading that much easier.

Once you become adept at reading, the hyphens within the Transliterated words should be ignored. To become adept at reciting these Hymns, please listen to them as you read/sing along.

सीताराम
सीताराम सीताराम
सीताराम सीताराम
सीताराम सीताराम

ॐ

सीताराम सीताराम सीताराम
सीताराम सीताराम सीताराम सीताराम सीताराम
सीताराम सीताराम सीताराम सीताराम सीताराम सीताराम

श्रीजानकीवल्लभो विजयते
śrījānakīvallabho vijayate

श्री हनुमान चालीसा
śrī-hanumāna-cālīsā

सीताराम सीताराम सीताराम सीताराम सीताराम सीताराम

दोहा - dohā

श्रीगुरु चरन सरोज रज निज मन मुकुर सुधारि ।
śrīguru carana saroja raja nija mana mukura sudhāri,
बरनऊँ रघुबर बिमल जस जो दायक फल चारि ॥
baranaūm̐ raghubara bimala jasa jo dāyaka phala cāri.

Trans:

Cleansing the mirror of my mind with the pollen dust from the lotus feet of the revered Guru, I sing the unsullied glories of Shrī Rāma—the bestower of the four fruits of life.

बुद्धि हीन तनु जानिकै सुमिरौं पवन कुमार ।
buddhi hīna tanu jānikai sumiraum̐ pavana kumāra,
बल बुद्धि बिद्या देहु मोहि हरहु कलेश विकार ॥
bala buddhi bidyā dehu mohi harahu kaleśa vikāra.

Trans:

Knowing this material body to be void of intelligence and seeped in ignorance, I meditate on the Son-of-Wind seeking his favor: Impart to me strength, intelligence, virtuosity; and remove all ailments and imperfections, my Lord.

चौपाई - caupāī

जय हनुमान ज्ञान गुण सागर । जय कपीश तिहुँ लोक उजागर ॥
jaya hanumāna jñāna guṇa sāgara, jaya kapīśa tihum̐ loka ujāgara. 1.

Trans:

Glory be to Hanumān—the ocean of wisdom and virtues. Victory to the monkey-god whose resplendency irradiates the three spheres of creation.

राम दूत अतुलित बल धामा । अंजनिपुत्र पवनसुत नामा ॥
rāma dūta atulita bala dhāmā, aṁjani-putra pavanasuta nāmā. 2.

Trans:

Glory be to the divine messenger and servant of Shrī Rāma, the repository of immeasurable strength. Glory be to mother Anjanī's boy, bearing the name Pavana-Suth—Son-of-Wind.

महाबीर बिक्रम बजरंगी । कुमति निवार सुमति के संगी ॥

mahābīra bikrama bajaraṁgī, kumati nivāra sumati ke saṁgī. 3.

Trans:

O supremely valorous hero of wondrous great deeds, with a body that is strong as diamond: evilness of the mind you cure; a companion you are of those with minds good and pure.

कंचन बरन बिराज सुबेषा । कानन कुंडल कुंचित केशा ॥

kaṁcana barana birāja subeṣā, kānana kuṁḍala kuṁcita keśā. 4.

Trans:

With a complexion that's molten gold, you shine resplendent in your exquisite form—with rings in your ears and lovely curly locks.

हाथ बज्र और ध्वजा बिराजै । काँधे मूँज जनेऊ साजै ॥

hātha bajra aura dhvajā birājai, kām̐dhe mūm̐ja janeū sājai. 5.

Trans:

In your hands are held a mace and a flag; and there's Munji and Janeu embellished across your shoulders, well adorned.

शङ्कर स्वयं केशरीनंदन । तेज प्रताप महा जग बंदन ॥

śaṅkara svayaṁ keśarīnaṁdana, teja pratāpa mahā jaga baṁdana. 6.

Trans:

You are Shankar himself (embodied as Hanuman), born to the mighty Kesharī—the delight of his heart; your majesty and prowess is astounding—venerated throughout the universe.

विद्यावान गुणी अति चातुर । राम काज करिबे को आतुर ॥

vidyā-vāna guṇī ati cātura, rāma kāja karibe ko ātura. 7.

Trans:

Learned in all the sciences, virtuous, most clever and wise—you are ever so eager to do all of Rāma's work.

प्रभु चरित्र सुनिबे को रसिया । राम लखन सीता मन बसिया ॥

prabhu caritra sunibe ko rasiyā, rāma lakhana sītā mana basiyā. 8.

Trans:

Your greatest delight is in listening to the glories of the Lord, and Rāma-Lakshman-Sītā ever reside in your heart; nay—you ever abide in the hearts of Lakshman-Sītā-Rāma.

सूक्ष्म रूप धरि सियहिं दिखावा । बिकट रूप धरि लंक जरावा ॥

sūkṣma rūpa dhari siyahiṁ dikhāvā, bikaṭa rūpa dhari laṁka jarāvā. 9.

भीम रूप धरि असुर सँहारे । रामचन्द्र के काज सँवारे ॥
bhīma rūpa dhari asura saṁhāre, rāma-candra ke kāja saṁvāre. 10.
Trans:
When visiting mother Sītā you showed yourself in tiny diminutive form; then growing to fearsome colossal size you burnt the whole of Lankā down; assuming a valorous form you destroyed many demons—thus you ever serve to facilitate the works of the Lord-God Shrī Rāma-Chandra.

लाय संजीवनि लखन जियाये । श्री रघुबीर हरषि उर लाये ॥
lāya saṁjīvani lakhana jiyāye, śrī raghu-bīra haraṣi ura lāye. 11.
Trans:
You brought the Sanjīvanī and brought Lakshman back to life—whereupon Shrī Rāma embraced you with a heart full of joy.

रघुपति कीन्ही बहुत बड़ाई । तुम मम प्रिय भरतहिं सम भाई ॥
raghupati kīnhī bahuta baṛāī, tuma mama priya bharatahiṁ sama bhāī. 12.
Trans:
Rāma, King of Raghus, extolled you profusely and then He proclaimed: You are to me just like Bharata, dear brother of mine.

सहस बदन तुम्हरो जस गावैं । अस कहि श्रीपति कंठ लगावैं ॥
sahasa badana tumharo jasa gāvaiṁ, asa kahi śrīpati kaṁṭha lagāvaiṁ. 13.
Trans:
Thousands of beings are singing your praise—with those words to you, Rāma again to you, unto His heart, did raise.

सनकादिक ब्रह्मादि मुनीशा । नारद शारद सहित अहीशा ॥
sanak-ādika brahmādi munīśā, nārada śārada sahita ahīśā. 14.
जम कुबेर दिगपाल जहाँ ते । कबि कोबिद कहि सके कहाँ ते ॥
jama kubera digapāla jahāṁ te, kabi kobida kahi sakai kahāṁ te. 15.
Trans:
Celibate Rishis like Sanaka; gods like Brahmmā; the foremost Munis; Nārad, Saraswatī with Shiva and Vishnu; the eight Dikpālas including Yama and Kubera—they all tell you glory but fail to fully delineate it; how then can mere mortals, poets and Vedic scholars sing your laurels?

तुम उपकार सुग्रीवहिं कीन्हा । राम मिलाय राज पद दीन्हा ॥
tuma upakāra sugrīvahiṁ kīnhā, rāma milāya rāja pada dīnhā. 16.
Trans:
You bestowed favor upon Sugrīva—you brought him near to Shri Rāma and made him the King of Kishkindhā.

तुम्हरो मंत्र बिभीषन माना । लंकेश्वर भए सब जग जाना ॥
tumharo maṁtra bibhīṣana mānā, laṁkeśvara bhae saba jaga jānā. 17.
Trans:

Vibhīshan accepted your Mantra, and as consequence became the King of Shri Lankā—this is well known throughout the world.

जुग सहस्त्र जोजन पर भानू । लील्यो ताहि मधुर फल जानू ॥

* juga sahastra jojana para bhānū, līlyo tāhi madhura phala jānū. 18.

Trans:

At a thousand Yuga Yojan is the Sun, and mistaking it for a sweet fruit, you supped it up—while you were still an infant.

प्रभु मुद्रिका मेलि मुख माहीं । जलधि लाँघि गये अचरज नाहीं ॥

prabhu mudrikā meli mukha māhīṁ, jaladhi lām̐ghi gaye acaraja nāhīṁ. 19.

Trans:

The ring of the Lord you placed in your mouth and then leaped across the ocean to give it to Sītā. But what wonder is there in that? [Verily, scaling the impossible comes to you with ease.]

दुर्गम काज जगत के जेते । सुगम अनुग्रह तुम्हरे तेते ॥

durgama kāja jagata ke jete, sugama anugraha tumhare tete. 20.

Trans:

All the difficult tasks of the world become easy were it your pleasure—if there, O Lord, be the favor of your grace.

राम दुआरे तुम रखवारे । होत न आज्ञा बिनु पैसारे ॥

rāma duāre tuma rakhavāre, hota na ājñā binu paisāre. 21.

Trans:

You are the keeper and protector of the gateway to Rāma; without your command, nobody can enter the abode of Shrī Rāma.

सब सुख लहैं तुम्हारी शरना । तुम रक्षक काहू को डर ना ॥

saba sukha lahaiṁ tumhārī śaranā, tuma rakṣaka kāhū ko ḍara nā. 22.

Trans:

Every happiness abides with those who bide under your protection. With you as one's guardian, there is never a cause of any fear.

आपन तेज सम्हारो आपै । तीनौं लोक हाँक ते काँपै ॥

āpana teja samhāro āpai, tīnauṁ loka hām̐ka te kām̐pai. 23.

Trans:

You alone can withstand your own splendor; verily the three worlds quake when your thunder.

भूत पिशाच निकट नहिं आवै । महाबीर जब नाम सुनावै ॥

bhūta piśāca nikaṭa nahiṁ āvai, mahābīra jaba nāma sunāvai. 24.

Trans:

Evil spirits and ghosts dare come near not—when the chant of Mahābira, your name, is invoked.

नासै रोग हरै सब पीरा । जपत निरंतर हनुमत बीरा ॥
nāsai roga harai saba pīrā, japata niraṁtara hanumata bīrā. 25.
Trans:
All diseases are destroyed, all pains are ended—with the constant chant of the Name 'Hanumān', the Mighty-Brave-Supreme.

संकट ते हनुमान छुड़ावै । मन क्रम बचन ध्यान जो लावै ॥
saṁkaṭa te hanumāna chuṛāvai, mana krama bacana dhyāna jo lāvai. 26.
Trans:
Lord Hanumān removes all afflictions, all adversities—for those who dwell on Hanumān through their heart, words and deeds.

सब पर राम तपस्वी राजा । तिन के काज सकल तुम साजा ॥
saba para rāma tapasvī rājā, tina ke kāja sakala tuma sājā. 27.
Trans:
Rāma, the Ascetic-King, is the sovereign ruler over all; and it is you who administer his works.

और मनोरथ जो कोउ लावै । तासु अमित जीवन फल पावै ॥
aura manoratha jo kou lāvai, tāsu amita jīvana phala pāvai. 28.
Trans:
When one comes before you with a heart's desire, you yield unto him unremitting fruits—for the whole life in entire.

चारों जुग परताप तुम्हारा । है परसिद्ध जगत उजियारा ॥
cāroṁ juga paratāpa tumhārā, hai parasiddha jagata ujiyārā. 29.
Trans:
Your resplendency persists across all Times; in all the four Yugas, your fame illumines throughout the universe.

साधु संत के तुम रखवारे । असुर निकंदन राम दुलारे ॥
sādhu saṁta ke tuma rakhavāre, asura nikaṁdana rāma dulāre. 30.
Trans:
You—dear-most (son) of Rāma—are the guardian of the saintly, virtuous, wise; and you are the destroyer of the fiends and the vile.

अष्ट सिद्धि नव निधि के दाता । अस बर दीन्ह जानकी माता ॥
aṣṭa siddhi nava nidhi ke dātā, asa bara dīnha jānakī mātā. 31.
Trans:
You are the bestower of all eight Siddhis and nine Nidhis—Mother Sītā, daughter of Janak, herself endowed you with that power.

राम रसायन तुम्हरे पासा । सदा रहउ रघुपति के दासा ॥
rāma rasāyana tumhare pāsā, sadā rahau raghupati ke dāsā. 32.
Trans:
You own the sweet treasure of devotion towards Shri Rāma; you ever abide as the foremost attendant of that Jewel of Raghu scion.

तुम्हरे भजन राम को पावै । जनम जनम के दुख बिसरावै ॥
tumhare bhajana rāma ko pāvai, janama janama ke dukha bisarāvai. 33.

अंत काल रघुबर पुर जाई । जहाँ जन्म हरिभक्त कहाई ॥
aṁta kāla raghubara pura jāī, jahām̐ janma haribhakta kahāī. 34.

Trans:

Through devotion to you, one is able to obtain to the Lord; and the adversities and afflictions of millions of births become defeated thereupon; and at the time of their end, one goes to Rāma's own abode—remaining there eternally as Rāma's very own.

और देवता चित्त न धरई । हनुमत सेइ सर्ब सुख करई ॥
aura devatā citta na dharaī, hanumata sei sarba sukha karaī. 35.

Trans:

Swearing by no other god and just serving Shrī Hanumān alone—one obtains every felicity in this world and the next.

संकट कटै मिटै सब पीरा । जो सुमिरै हनुमत बलबीरा ॥
saṁkaṭa kaṭai miṭai saba pīrā, jo sumirai hanumata balabīrā. 36.

Trans:

All troubles are cut short, all pains removed—for those who meditate upon Shri Hanumān, the mighty, brave, supreme.

जय जय जय हनुमान गोसाईं । कृपा करहु गुरु देव की नाईं ॥
jaya jaya jaya hanumāna gosāīṁ, kṛpā karahu guru deva kī nāīṁ. 37.

Trans:

Victory to you O Hanumān, O master of senses. May you remain ever victorious, ever triumphant. And do plese shower your grace upon us—as lovingly as a Guru does.

यह शत बार पाठ कर जोई । छूटै बंदि महा सुख सोई ॥
yaha śata bāra pāṭha kara joī, chūṭai baṁdi mahā sukha soī. 38.

Trans:

One who recites this Hanumān Chālīsā a hundred times is released from all bondages and obtains bliss everlasting.

जो यह पढ़ै हनुमान चालीसा । होय सिद्धि साखी गौरीसा ॥
jo yaha paṛhai hanumāna cālīsā, hoya siddhi sākhī gaurīsā. 39.

Trans:

One who reads this Hanumān Chālīsā becomes a Siddha (Master)—Gaurī's Lord Shiva himself bears witness to that.

तुलसीदास सदा हरि चेरा । कीजै नाथ हृदय महँ डेरा ॥

tulasī-dāsa sadā hari cerā, kījai nātha hṛdaya mahaṁ ḍerā. 40.

Trans:

Tulsīdās is ever a humble disciple of Shrī Rāma; O Lord Hanumān, do please take up thy abode in my heart as well (since Rāma is already there).

दोहा · dohā

पवन तनय संकट हरन मंगल मूरति रूप ।

pavana tanaya saṁkaṭa harana maṁgala mūrati rūpa,

राम लखन सीता सहित हृदय बसहु सुर भूप ॥

rāma lakhana sītā sahita hṛdaya basahu sura bhūpa.

Trans:

O Son-of-Wind—O remover of all disasters and sins—O Radiant-One of the most auspicious visage—may you ever and ever abide in my heart—along with Sītā, Lakshman, Rāma—O first amongst the gods.

* The distance to Sun (***Bhānū)*** is being given out in the 18th Chaupai as 96 million miles (12,000x1000x8). ***Juga*** (which equal 12,000 Divine-Years as per Vedic-Time-Scale) is used as a number here; ***sahastra*** means 1000; ***jojana*** is a distance of 8 miles. This distance to Sun—which is within 3.3% of modern day calculations—in mere three simple words ***(juga sahastra jojana)***, given out by Tulsīdās from sixteenth century India, is remarkable; for it not only shows what all our ancients knew way, way back; but it also demonstrates Tulsīdās' dexterity in choosing the right succinct words throughout his poesy.

(Author of this Original Devanāgri Hymn is: Goswamī Tulsīdās [16th Century Saint]. Translator: Sushma)

सीताराम
सीताराम सीताराम
सीताराम सीताराम
सीताराम सीताराम

ॐ

श्री गणेशाय नमः

OM śrī gaṇeśāya namaḥ

श्रीजानकीवल्लभो विजयते

śrījānakīvallabho vijayate

श्रीरामरक्षास्तोत्र

śrī-rāma-rakṣā-stotra

सीताराम सीताराम सीताराम सीताराम सीताराम

अस्य श्रीरामरक्षास्तोत्रमन्त्रस्य बुधकौशिक ऋषिः
asya śrī-rāma-rakṣāstotra-mantrasya budha-kauśika ṛṣiḥ

श्रीसीतारामचन्द्रो देवता अनुष्टुप् छन्दः
śrī-sītā-rāma-candro devatā anuṣṭup chandaḥ

सीता शक्तिः श्रीमान् हनुमान् कीलकं
sītā śaktiḥ śrīmān hanumān kīlakaṁ

श्रीरामचन्द्रप्रीत्यर्थे रामरक्षास्तोत्रजपे विनियोगः ॥
śrī-rāma-candra-prītyarthe rāma-rakṣā-stotra-jape viniyogaḥ .

Trans:

Of this Rāmrakshāstotra (**Hymn-of-Rāma**—for gaining **Protection**) the *Rishi* is: Buddha-Kaushik; the eight syllable quarter *Anushthap* is: the Meter; and the Deity: **Shrī Sītā-Ramachandra**. **Shrī Sītā** is the underlying energy: *Shakti*; and **Shrī Hanumān**: the anchor; the usage is: Recitation. This Rāmrakshāstotra is invoked through recitation—to please Shrī Ramachandra and earn His benediction and grace.

-- *अथ ध्यानम्* . *atha dhyānam* --

-- [**Meditate**] --

ध्यायेदाजानुबाहुं धृतशरधनुषं बद्धपद्मासनस्थं
dhyāye-dājānu-bāhuṁ dhṛta-śara-dhanuṣaṁ baddha-padmā-sanasthaṁ

पीतं वासो वसानं नवकमलदलस्पर्धिनेत्रं प्रसन्नम् ।
pītaṁ vāso vasānaṁ nava-kamala-dala-spardhi-netraṁ prasannam ,

वामाङ्कारूढसीतामुखकमलमिलल्लोचनं नीरदाभं
vāmāṅka-rūḍha-sītā-mukha-kamala-mila-llocanaṁ nīra-dābhaṁ

नानालंकारदीप्तं दधतमुरुजटामण्डलं रामचन्द्रम् ॥
nānā-laṁkāra-dīptaṁ dadhata-murujaṭā-maṇḍalaṁ rāma-candram .

Trans:

Meditate upon Him: of abundant arms, holding bow and arrows in His hands, donning yellow apparels, seated in a lotus posture; of a beaming countenance, whose exquisite eyes—which compete with the petals of fresh lotus—are locked on the lovely lotus-faced Sītā sitting to his left. Upon Him—of a hue dark as heavy rain-clouds, crowned with long dense matted hair, who shines resplendent with several ornaments—upon Him, Bhagwan Shrī Ramachandra, meditate.

-- इति ध्यानम् . *iti dhyānam* --

-- [Meditation concludes (Mantras Begin)] --

चरितं रघुनाथस्य शतकोटि प्रविस्तरम् ।

caritaṁ raghu-nāthasya śata-koṭi pravis-taram ,

एकैकमक्षरं पुंसां महापातकनाशनम् ॥ १ ॥

ek-aikam-akṣaraṁ puṁsāṁ mahā-pātaka-nāśa-nam . 1 .

Trans:

Illimitable the resplendent glory of Raghunāth, a hundred billion words in extent—each and every word of which destructs the most grievous sin.

ध्यात्वा नीलोत्पलश्यामं रामं राजीवलोचनम् ।

dhyā-tvā nīl-otpala-śyāmaṁ rāmaṁ rājīva-locanam ,

जानकीलक्ष्मणोपेतं जटामुकुटमण्डितम् ॥ २ ॥

jānakī-lakṣmaṇo-petaṁ jaṭā-mukuṭa-maṇḍitam . 2 .

सासितूणधनुर्बाणपाणिं नक्तंचरान्तकम् ।

sāsitūṇa-dhanur-bāṇa-pāṇiṁ naktaṁ-carāntakam ,

स्वलीलया जगत्त्रातुमविर्भूतमजं विभुम् ॥ ३ ॥

sva-līlayā jagat-trātuma-virbhūta-majaṁ vibhum . 3 .

रामरक्षां पठेत्प्राज्ञः पापघ्नीं सर्वकामदाम् ।

rāma-rakṣāṁ paṭhet-prājñaḥ pāpa-ghnīṁ sarva-kāma-dām ,

शिरो मे राघवः पातु भालं दशरथात्मजः ॥ ४ ॥

śiro me rāghavaḥ pātu bhālaṁ daśarath-ātmajaḥ . 4 .

Trans:

Meditating upon Him—of a hue that is a dark blue, with eyes like a pair of lotuses, well-adorned with a crown of matted hair; who wields sword, bow and arrows, the destroyer of demons; who, though birthless, of his own will became Incarnate to protect the world—meditating upon Him: Shrī Rāma accompanied by Sītā and Lakshman—the wise recite this Rāmrakshāstotra—which destroys all sins, grants every desire, and bestows God's protection. Now then I pray: May Rāghav guard the head; may Dasharatha's son protect the forehead.

कौसल्येयो दृशौ पातु विश्वामित्रप्रियः श्रुती ।
kausal-yeyo dṛśau pātu viśvā-mitra-priyaḥ śrutī ,
घ्राणं पातु मखत्राता मुखं सौमित्रिवत्सलः ॥ ५ ॥
ghrāṇaṁ pātu makha-trātā mukhaṁ saumitri-vatsalaḥ . 5 .

Trans:
May the eyes stand protected by the son of Kausalyā; the ears by the favorite disciple of Vishwāmitra; the nasals by the savior of sacrificial fires; the mouth by Him who is most affectionate to the son of Sumitrā.

जिह्वां विद्यानिधिः पातु कण्ठं भरतवंदितः ।
jihvāṁ vidyā-nidhiḥ pātu kaṇṭhaṁ bharata-vaṁditaḥ ,
स्कन्धौ दिव्यायुधः पातु भुजौ भग्नेशकार्मुकः ॥ ६ ॥
skandhau divyā-yudhaḥ pātu bhujau bhag-neśa-kārmukaḥ . 6 .

Trans:
May the ocean-of-wisdom protect the tongue; Bharat's Lord the neck. May the wielder of celestial weapons shield the shoulders; may the arms be fortified by His mighty arms who effortlessly broke the Bow of Shankara.

करौ सीतापतिः पातु हृदयं जामदग्न्यजित् ।
karau sītā-patiḥ pātu hṛdayaṁ jāma-dagnya-jit ,
मध्यं पातु खरध्वंसी नाभिं जाम्बवदाश्रयः ॥ ७ ॥
madhyaṁ pātu khara-dhvaṁsī nābhiṁ jāmbavad-āśrayaḥ . 7 .

Trans:
May the Lord of Sītā protect the hands; may He, who won over Parshurām, protect the heart; may the middle be preserved by the slayer of demon Khara; may He, who gave shelter to Jāmvant, shelter the navel.

सुग्रीवेशः कटी पातु सक्थिनी हनुमत्प्रभुः ।
sugrī-veśaḥ kaṭī pātu sakthinī hanumat-prabhuḥ ,
ऊरू रघूत्तमः पातु रक्षःकुलविनाशकृत् ॥ ८ ॥
ūrū raghū-ttamaḥ pātu rakṣaḥ-kula-vināśakṛt . 8 .

Trans:
May the Master of Sugrīva protects the waist; may the Lord of Hanumān protect the hips. May the laps stand protected by the best of Raghus scion—who is the destroyer of lineage of demons.

जानुनी सेतुकृत्पातु जङ्घे दशमुखान्तकः ।
jānunī setu-kṛtpātu jaṅaghe daśa-mukh-āntakaḥ ,
पादौ बिभीषणश्रीदः पातु रामोऽखिलं वपुः ॥ ९ ॥
pādau bibhīṣaṇ-aśrīdaḥ pātu rām-o'khilaṁ vapuḥ . 9 .

Trans:

May He, who spanned a bridge across the sea—guard the knees; may the slayer of the Ten-Headed demon—protect the shins; may the bestower of kingdom to Vibhīshan—protect the feet. May Shrī Rāma be the armor of the entire body.

एतां रामबलोपेतां रक्षां यः सुकृती पठेत् ।
etāṁ rāma-balo-petāṁ rakṣāṁ yaḥ sukṛtī paṭhet ,
स चिरायुः सुखी पुत्री विजयी विनयी भवेत् ॥ १० ॥
sa cirāyuḥ sukhī putrī vijayī vinayī bhavet . 10 .

Trans:
Blessed souls who recite this Hymn—replete with the potency of Lord Rāma—lead long prosperous lives, fortified full of blessings: such as longevity, happiness, progeny, humility, success.

पातालभूतलव्योमचारिणश्छद्मचारिणः ।
pātāla-bhūtala-vyoma-cāriṇa-śchadma-cāriṇaḥ ,
न द्रष्टुमपि शक्तास्ते रक्षितं रामनामभिः ॥ ११ ॥
na draṣṭu-mapi śakt-āste rakṣitaṁ rāma-nāma-bhiḥ . 11 .

Trans:
Evil spirits that travel secretly changing forms—the hidden wanderers of earth, heaven, and hell—can not even catch a glimpse of those who stand protected by the power of the chant of Rāma-Nāma.

रामेति रामभद्रेति रामचन्द्रेति वा स्मरन् ।
rāmeti rāma-bhadreti rāma-candreti vā smaran ,
नरो न लिप्यते पापैर्भुक्तिं मुक्तिं च विन्दति ॥ १२ ॥
naro na lipyate pāpai-bhuktiṁ muktiṁ ca vindati . 12 .

Trans:
People who continually reflect upon His names: like Rāma, Rāmbhadra, Rāmachandra, never get entangled in sin; and with ease they attain the aim of their choosing—be it final emancipation, or a zestful worldly life.

जगज्जैत्रेकमन्त्रेण रामनाम्नाऽभिरक्षितम् ।
jagajjai-trekam-antreṇa rāma-nāmnā-'bhirakṣ-itam ,
यः कण्ठे धारयेत्तस्य करस्थाः सर्वसिद्धयः ॥ १३ ॥
yaḥ kaṇṭhe dhāra-yettasya kara-sthāḥ sarva-siddha-yaḥ . 13 .

Trans:
They who wear on their neck [memorize] this Hymn—the sole world-winning Mantra—get all *Siddhis* (supernatural powers) within their grasp.

वज्रपंजरनामेदं यो रामकवचं स्मरेत् ।
vajra-paṁjara-nāmedaṁ yo rāma-kavacaṁ smaret ,

अव्याहताज्ञः सर्वत्र लभते जयमंगलम् ॥ १४ ॥

avyā-hatā-jñaḥ sarvatra labhate jaya-maṁgalam . 14 .

Trans:

Those who stand fortified by this Armor of Rāma—known as the Cage of Diamond—command obedience over all; and they remain ever victorious, ever bright, ever auspicious.

आदिष्टवान्यथा स्वप्ने रामरक्षामिमां हरः ।

ādiṣṭa-vānyathā svapne rāma-rakṣā-mimāṁ haraḥ ,

तथा लिखितवान्प्रातः प्रभुद्धो बुधकौशिकः ॥ १५ ॥

tathā likhita-vān-prātaḥ pra-bhuddho budha-kauśikaḥ . 15 .

Trans:

It was in a revelation that this protective Shield-of-Rāma was divulged by Lord Shiva; and upon waking it was transcribed by Buddha-Kaushik as ordained.

आरामः कल्पवृक्षाणां विरामः सकलापदाम् ।

ārāmaḥ kalpa-vṛkṣāṇāṁ virā-maḥ sakal-āpadām ,

अभिरामस्त्रिलोकानां रामः श्रीमान्स नः प्रभुः ॥ १६ ॥

abhirāmas-trilok-ānāṁ rāmaḥ śrī-mānsa naḥ prabhuḥ . 16 .

Trans:

He—who is the destroyer of every obstacle—who is, as it were, a grove of wish-yielding trees—who is the praise of all the three worlds—He Shrī Rāma—is our Bhagwān, Lord-God Supreme.

तरुणौ रूपसम्पन्नौ सुकुमारौ महाबलौ ।

taruṇau rūpa-sampannau su-kumārau mahā-balau ,

पुण्डरीकविशालाक्षौ चीरकृष्णाजिनाम्बरौ ॥ १७ ॥

puṇḍarīka-viśāl-ākṣau cīra-kṛṣṇā-jinām-barau . 17 .

फलमूलाशिनौ दान्तौ तापसौ ब्रह्मचारिणौ ।

phala-mūl-āśinau dāntau tāpasau brahma-cāriṇau ,

पुत्रौ दशरथस्यैतौ भ्रातरौ रामलक्ष्मणौ ॥ १८ ॥

putrau daśa-ratha-syaitau bhrā-tarau rāma-lakṣmaṇau . 18 .

शरण्यौ सर्वसत्त्वानां श्रेष्ठौ सर्वधनुष्मताम् ।

śaraṇ-yau sarva-satt-vānāṁ śre-ṣṭhau sarva-dhanuṣ-matām ,

रक्षः कुलनिहन्तारौ त्रायेतां नो रघूत्तमौ ॥ १९ ॥

rakṣaḥ kulani-hantārau trā-yetāṁ no raghū-ttamau . 19 .

Trans:

Full of beauty, charming youths mighty and strong, with lotus-like broad exquisite eyes, who have donned the bark of tree and dark deer skins, who subsist on fruits and roots, who live as celibates practicing penance, those sons of Dashrath—the two brothers Rāma and Lakshman—the foremost amongst all archers, the destroyers of whole race of demons, who give life and shelter to all beings—those best of scions of Raghus, may they grant protection to me.

आत्तसज्जधनुषाविषुस्पृशावक्षयाशुगनिषङ्गसङ्गनौ ।
ātta-sajja-dhanuṣā-viṣu-spṛśā-vakṣay-āśuga-niṣaṅga-saṅganau ,
रक्षणाय मम रामलक्ष्मणावग्रतः पथि सदैव गच्छताम् ॥ २० ॥
rakṣ-aṇāya mama rāma-lakṣmaṇ-āvagrataḥ pathi sadaiva gacch-atām . 20 .

Trans:
Accompanying me, with bows pulled and ready, with their hand stroking the arrows, with quivers full of unfailing arms slung on their back—may those wayfarers Rāma and Lakshman always stay in the front—as I traverse my path—granting their protective care.

संनद्धः कवची खड्गी चापबाणधरो युवा ।
saṁ-naddhaḥ kavacī khaḍgī cāpa-bāṇa-dharo yuvā ,
गच्छन्मनोरथान्नश्च रामः पातु सलक्ष्मणः ॥ २१ ॥
gacchan-manorath-ānnaśca rāmaḥ pātu sa-lakṣmaṇaḥ . 21 .

Trans:
Always prepared and armored—armed with bows, arrows, swords—of youthful forms—may Rāma and Lakshman always abide ahead of me, protecting my cherished thoughts.

रामो दाशरथिः शूरो लक्ष्मणानुचरो बली ।
rāmo dāśarathiḥ śūro lakṣmaṇ-ānucaro balī ,
काकुत्स्थः पुरुषः पूर्णः कौसल्येयो रघूत्तमः ॥ २२ ॥
kākuts-thaḥ puruṣaḥ pūrṇaḥ kausal-yeyo raghū-ttamaḥ . 22 .
वेदान्तवेद्यो यज्ञेशः पुराणपुरुषोत्तमः ।
vedānta-vedyo yajñ-eśaḥ purāṇa-puruṣ-ottamaḥ ,
जानकीवल्लभः श्रीमान् अप्रमेय पराक्रमः ॥ २३ ॥
jānakī-vallabh-aḥ śrī-mān a-prameya parā-kramaḥ . 23 .
इत्येतानि जपन्नित्यं मद्भक्तः श्रद्धयान्वितः ।
itye-tāni japan-nityaṁ mad-bhaktaḥ śraddha-yānvitaḥ ,
अश्वमेधाधिकं पुण्यं सम्प्राप्नोति न संशयः ॥ २४ ॥
aśva-medhā-dhikaṁ puṇyaṁ sam-prāp-noti na saṁś-ayaḥ . 24 .

Trans:
Rāma, Dāsharathī [Dasharath's son], Shūro [Brave], Lakshman-anucharo [whom Lakshman follows], Balī [Powerful], Kākutstha [Kakutstha's Descendent], Purusha

[the Supreme-Reality beyond Māyā], Pūrna [Complete], Kausalyeyo [Kausalyā's son], Raghūttama [Best of Raghus], Vedānta-Vedyo [Import of Vedanta], Yagyesha [Lord of Yagya], Purāṇa [Ancient-Most], Purushottama [Supreme-Most], Jānakī-Vallabha [Sītā's Beloved], Shrīmān [Lord of Prosperity], Aprameya-Parākrami [Immeasurably-Brave]—they who recites these names of Rāma everyday with faith, such devotees of mine will assuredly get the fruit of Ashwamegha Yagya and more—of this let there be no doubt [says Lord Shankar].

रामं दुर्वादलश्यामं पद्माक्षं पीतवाससम् ।
rāmaṁ durvā-dala-śyāmaṁ padm-ākṣaṁ pīta-vāsa-sam ,
स्तुवन्ति नामभिर्दिव्यैर्न ते संसारिणो नराः ॥ २५ ॥
stu-vanti nāmabhir-div-yairna te saṁ-sāriṇo narāḥ . 25 .

Trans:

Chanting these divine names and singing the praises of Shrī Rāma—He, who wears yellow raiments, the lotus-eyed Lord of dark complexion, of a swarthy hue as the leaves of dark *Doorba*—the faithful are never anymore trapped in the cycle of transmigration.

रामं लक्ष्मणपूर्वजं रघुवरं सीतापतिं सुन्दरं
rāmaṁ lakṣmaṇa-pūrvajaṁ raghu-varaṁ sītā-patiṁ sundaraṁ
काकुत्स्थं करुणार्णवं गुणनिधिं विप्रप्रियं धार्मिकम् ।
kākut-sthaṁ karuṇār-ṇavaṁ guṇa-nidhiṁ vipra-priyaṁ dhārmikam ,
राजेन्द्रं सत्यसंधं दशरथतनयं श्यामलं शान्तमूर्तिं
rājendraṁ satya-saṁdhaṁ daśaratha-tanayaṁ śyāmalaṁ śānta-mūrtiṁ
वन्दे लोकाभिरामं रघुकुलतिलकं राघवं रावणारिम् ॥ २६ ॥
vande lok-ābhirāmaṁ raghu-kula-tilakaṁ rāghavaṁ rāvaṇā-rim . 26 .

Trans:

Unto Rāma—the revered of Lakshman, the best of the House of Raghus, the most-charming Lord of Sītā, the ocean of compassion, the scion of Kakustha, a treasurehouse of virtues, the darling of the virtuous, most religious and wise, the Sovereign King of Kings, conjoined to Truth, the dark-complexioned son of Dashrath, Embodied-Bliss, the most exquisite in creation, the crown jewel of Raghus, slayer of the demon Rāvan—unto Him, Lord Rāghav, my repeated salutations.

रामाय रामभद्राय रामचन्द्राय वेधसे ।
rāmāya rāma-bhadrāya rāma-candrāya vedhase ,
रघुनाथाय नाथाय सीतायाः पतये नमः ॥ २७ ॥
raghu-nāthāya nāthāya sītāyāḥ pataye namaḥ . 27 .

Trans:

I bow to Rāma; my obeisance to Rāmabhadra; my many venerations to Rāmachandra, the omniscient Lord-God Raghunāth; again and again my repeated salutations to Sītāpatī—the Lord of Sītā.

श्रीराम राम रघुनन्दन राम राम
śrīrāma rāma raghu-nandana rāma rāma
श्रीराम राम भरताग्रज राम राम ।
śrīrāma rāma bharat-āgraja rāma rāma ,
श्रीराम राम रणकर्कश राम राम
śrīrāma rāma raṇa-karkaśa rāma rāma
श्रीराम राम शरणं भव राम राम ॥ २८ ॥
śrīrāma rāma śaraṇaṁ bhava rāma rāma . 28 .

Trans:

I stand in surrender to Shrī Rāma—Rāma, Rāma, Raghunandan [Raghu Scion] Rāma. I give myself unto Shrī Rāma—Rāma, Rāma, Bharatāgraja [Bharat's Elder] Rāma. I lay my life before Shrī Rāma—Rāma, Rāma, Rankarkasha [Terrible in Battle] Rāma. I take shelter in you O Rāma—Shrī Rāma, Rāma, Rāma; be my refuge, Lord-God.

श्रीरामचन्द्रचरणौ मनसा स्मरामि
śrī-rāma-candra-caraṇau manasā smarāmi
श्रीरामचन्द्रचरणौ वचसा गृणामि ।
śrī-rāma-candra-caraṇau vacasā gṛṇāmi ,
श्रीरामचन्द्रचरणौ शिरसा नमामि
śrī-rāma-candra-caraṇau śirasā namāmi
श्रीरामचन्द्रचरणौ शरणं प्रपद्ये ॥ २९ ॥
śrī-rāma-candra-caraṇau śaraṇaṁ prapadye . 29 .

Trans:

With my heart I reverence the feet of Shrī Rāmachandra. With my speech I make veneration to the holy feet of Shrī Rāmachandra. With my head I salute the sacred feet of Shrī Rāma. Bowing low I take complete refuge at the holy feet of Rāma—who is the cooling Moon to the burning flames of the world.

माता रामो मत्पिता रामचन्द्रः
mātā rāmo mat-pitā rāma-candraḥ
स्वामी रामो मत्सखा रामचन्द्रः ।
svāmī rāmo mat-sakhā rāma-candraḥ ,

सर्वस्वं मे रामचन्द्रो दयालु
sarva-svaṁ me rāma-candro dayālu
र्नान्यं जाने नैव जाने न जाने ॥ ३० ॥
rnā-nyaṁ jāne naiva jāne na jāne . 30 .

Trans:
Rāma is my loving mother, and Rāma my protective father. Rāma is my gracious Lord, and Rāma my beloved friend. My everyone and everything is only Rāmachandra, the most-compassionate Lord. Other than Rāma I know of no other—absolutely, I know of no one except Shrī Rāma.

दक्षिणे लक्ष्मणो यस्य वामे च जनकात्मजा ।
dakṣiṇe lakṣmaṇo yasya vāme ca janak-ātmajā ,
पुरतो मारुतिर्यस्य तं वन्दे रघुनन्दनम् ॥ ३१ ॥
purato mārutir-yasya taṁ vande raghu-nandanam . 31 .

Trans:
Who has Lakshmana to his right, and the daughter of Janaka to his left; before whom Hanumān is bowing down in reverence—to that Lord Raghu-Nandan I make my obeisance.

लोकाभिरामं रणरङ्गधीरं
lokā-bhirāmaṁ raṇa-raṅga-dhīraṁ
राजीवनेत्रं रघुवंशनाथम् ।
rājīva-netraṁ raghu-vaṁśa-nātham ,
कारुण्यरूपं करुणाकरं तं
kāruṇy-arūpaṁ karuṇā-karaṁ taṁ
श्रीरामचन्द्रं शरणं प्रपद्ये ॥ ३२ ॥
śrī-rāma-candraṁ śaraṇaṁ pra-padye . 32 .

Trans:
The cynosure of eyes of all beings, the most valiant in battle, the lotus-eyed Lord of the Raghu-Lineage, the embodiment of compassion—unto that Lord-God Rāmachandra, in complete surrender I approach.

मनोजवं मारुततुल्यवेगं
mano-javaṁ māruta-tulya-vegaṁ
जितेन्द्रियं बुद्धिमतां वरिष्ठम् ।
jit-endriyaṁ buddhi-matāṁ vari-ṣṭham ,
वातात्मजं वानरयूथमुख्यं
vāt-ātmajaṁ vānara-yūtha-mukhyaṁ

श्रीरामदूतं शरणं प्रपद्ये ॥ ३३ ॥
śrī-rāma-dūtaṁ śaraṇaṁ pra-padye . 33 .

Trans:

Who is quick as the mind and equal to his sire (the Wind) in speed—unto him—who is the master of his senses and the foremost amongst the wise, unto him—the Son-of-Wind, the chief of monkey hosts—unto that messenger of Lord Rāma—Shrī Hanumān, I come seeking refuge.

कूजन्तं रामरामेति मधुरं मधुराक्षरम् ।
kū-jantaṁ rāma-rāmeti madhuraṁ madhu-rākṣaram ,
आरुह्य कविताशाखां वन्दे वाल्मीकिकोकिलम् ॥ ३४ ॥
āruhya kavitā-śākhāṁ vande vālmīki-kokilam . 34 .

Trans:

He—who sports in the woods of the glories of Sītā-Rāma like a koel, who is ever singing the sweet name of Rāma sitting on the branches of poesy—to him, the grand sage Vālmiki, I offer my salutations.

आपदामपहर्तारं दातारं सर्वसम्पदाम् ।
āpadā-mapa-hartāraṁ dātā-raṁ sarva-sampadām ,
लोकाभिरामं श्रीरामं भूयो भूयो नमाम्यहम् ॥ ३५ ॥
lokā-bhirāmaṁ śrī-rāmaṁ bhūyo bhūyo namām-yaham . 35 .

Trans:

Unto Shrī Rāma—who takes away all the perils and difficulties of life, who is the granter of all wishes and prosperities, who is the most beloved of all beings in the world—I bow; and I bow repeatedly.

भर्जनं भवबीजानामर्जनं सुखसम्पदाम् ।
bhar-janaṁ bhava-bījā-nāmar-janaṁ sukha-sam-padām ,
तर्जनं यमदूतानां रामरामेति गर्जनम् ॥ ३६ ॥
tar-janaṁ yama-dūtā-nāṁ rāma-rāmeti gar-janam . 36 .

Trans:

The chants of the name of 'Rāma' is the fiery thunder which destructs the seed of the cycle of transmigration; it is the bestower of all felicity and wealth; and it puts fear even into the heart of the messenger-of-death.

रामो राजमणिः सदा विजयते रामं रमेशं भजे
rāmo rāja-maṇiḥ sadā vijayate rāmaṁ rameśaṁ bhaje
रामेणाभिहता निशाचरचमू रामाय तस्मै नमः ।
rāmeṇ-ābhihatā niśā-cara-camū rāmāya tasmai namaḥ ,
रामान्नास्ति परायणं परतरं रामस्य दासोऽस्म्यहं
rāmān-nāsti parā-yaṇaṁ parataraṁ rāmasya dāso-'smyahaṁ

रामे चित्तलयः सदा भवतु मे भो राम मामुद्धर ॥ ३७ ॥

rāme citta-layaḥ sadā bhavatu me bho rāma mām-uddhara . 37 .

Trans:

Rāma, the Crest-Jewel of Monarchs, is ever victorious; I sing the praises of Shrī Rāma, Lord of all beings. He Rāma, who decimated the whole army of night-roving demons, Him I devoutly revere. There is no greater refuge than Shrī Rāma; I am a servant of Shrī Rāma; my mind remains ever absorbed in Shrī Rāma. O Rāma, Lord-God Shrī Rāma, please redeem me.

राम रामेति रामेति रमे रामे मनोरमे ।

rāma rāmeti rāmeti rame rāme mano-rame ,

सहस्त्रनाम तत्तुल्यं रामनाम वरानने ॥ ३८ ॥

sahasra-nāma tat-tulyaṁ rāma-nāma varā-nane . 38 .

Trans:

Rāma, Rāma, Rāma—chanting this beautiful Name Rāma, my mind remains ever absorbed in God. The one name 'Rāma' is equivalent to a thousand other names of God, O fair-faced [Umā—says Shiva].

॥ इति श्रीबुधकौशिकमुनिविरचितं श्रीरामरक्षास्तोत्रं सम्पूर्णम् ॥

. iti śrī-budha-kauśika-muni-viraci-taṁ śrī-rāma-rakṣā-stotraṁ sam-pūrṇam .

— Thus ends the Rāmrakshāstotra composed by Shrī Buddha-Kaushik Muni —

(Author of this Original Sanskrit Hymn is: Buddha-Kaushik Muni [Pre-historic Sage]. Translator: Sushma)

सीताराम
सीताराम सीताराम
सीताराम सीताराम
सीताराम सीताराम

ॐ

श्री गणेशाय नमः
OM śrī gaṇeśāya namaḥ
श्रीजानकीवल्लभो विजयते
śrījānakīvallabho vijayate

श्रीकाकभुसुंडिरामायण
śrī-kāka-bhusuṁḍi-rāmāyaṇa

सीताराम सीताराम सीताराम सीताराम सीताराम सीताराम

दोहा-dohā:

नाथ कृतारथ भयउँ मैं तव दरसन खगराज ।
nātha kṛtāratha bhayauṁ maiṁ tava darasana khagarāja,
आयसु देहु सो करौं अब प्रभु आयहु केहि काज ॥६३क॥
āyasu dehu so karauṁ aba prabhu āyahu kehi kāja. 63(ka).

सदा कृतारथ रूप तुम्ह कह मृदु बचन खगेस ।
sadā kṛtāratha rūpa tumha kaha mṛdu bacana khagesa,
जेहि कै अस्तुति सादर निज मुख कीन्हि महेस ॥६३ख॥
jehi kai astuti sādara nija mukha kīnhi mahesa. 63(kha).

Trans:

[Bhushuṁdi addressed Garuda:] "I am blest by your sight; and now that I have seen you, O king of birds, please allow me to be of service to you. Pray say—what is the object of your visit my Lord?" "You are ever a picture of blessedness," replied Garuda in gracious tones, "seeing that Shiva, with his own mouth, reverently sings your praises.

चौपाई-caupāī:

सुनहु तात जेहि कारन आयउँ । सो सब भयउ दरस तव पायउँ ॥
sunahu tāta jehi kārana āyauṁ, so saba bhayau darasa tava pāyauṁ.
देखि परम पावन तव आश्रम । गयउ मोह संसय नाना भ्रम ॥
dekhi parama pāvana tava āśrama, gayau moha saṁsaya nānā bhrama.
अब श्रीराम कथा अति पावनि । सदा सुखद दुख पुंज नसावनि ॥
aba śrīrāma kathā ati pāvani, sadā sukhada dukha puṁja nasāvani.
सादर तात सुनावहु मोही । बार बार बिनवउँ प्रभु तोही ॥
sādara tāta sunāvahu mohī, bāra bāra binavauṁ prabhu tohī.
सुनत गरुड़ कै गिरा बिनीता । सरल सुप्रेम सुखद सुपुनीता ॥
sunata garuṛa kai girā binītā, sarala suprema sukhada supunītā.

भयउ तासु मन परम उछाहा । लाग कहै रघुपति गुन गाहा ॥
bhayau tāsu mana parama uchāhā, lāga kahai raghupati guna gāhā.
प्रथमहिं अति अनुराग भवानी । रामचरित सर कहेसि बखानी ॥
prathamahiṁ ati anurāga bhavānī, rāmacarita sara kahesi bakhānī.
पुनि नारद कर मोह अपारा । कहेसि बहुरि रावन अवतारा ॥
puni nārada kara moha apārā, kahesi bahuri rāvana avatārā.
प्रभु अवतार कथा पुनि गाई । तब सिसु चरित कहेसि मन लाई ॥
prabhu avatāra kathā puni gāī, taba sisu carita kahesi mana lāī.

Trans:

Hearken sire, the object for which I came has already been accomplished—and now I also have the privilege of being favored by your holy sight. Directly as I beheld this most consecrated hermitage of yours, my delusion came to an end—with all my distracting doubts gone. Now father please repeat to me with all solemnity the most sanctifying story of Shrī Rāma, which is ever delightful and a remedy for every ill—this, my Lord, is what I beg of you in all earnestness." On hearing Garuda's prayer—so humble sincere and affectionate, so graceful and pious—a supreme joy was diffused over the crow's soul, and he commenced the recital of Raghupatī's glories. First of all, O Bhawānī, he expounded with fervent devotion the glories of Rāma & Rāmcharitmanas & the cause of Incarnation of the Lord. He told of Nārad's great delusion and of Rāvan's advent. After this he versified the episode of the Lord's birth and then with diligence recounted the childish frolics of the Lord when He was an infant.

दोहा-dohā:

बालचरित कहि बिबिधि बिधि मन महँ परम उछाह ।
bālacarita kahi bibidhi bidhi mana mahaṁ parama uchāha,
रिषि आगवन कहेसि पुनि श्रीरघुबीर बिबाह ॥ ६४ ॥
riṣi āgavana kahesi puni śrīraghubīra bibāha. 64.

Trans:

After narrating all the varied details of Rāma's boyish sports with the utmost rapture of soul, he next spoke of Rishī Vishwāmitra's coming, and thereafter sketched out the marriage ceremonies of Raghubīr.

चौपाई-caupāī:

बहुरि राम अभिषेक प्रसंगा । पुनि नृप बचन राज रस भंगा ॥
bahuri rāma abhiṣeka prasaṁgā, puni nṛpa bacana rāja rasa bhaṁgā.
पुरबासिन्ह कर बिरह बिषादा । कहेसि राम लछिमन संबादा ॥
purabāsinha kara biraha biṣādā, kahesi rāma lachimana saṁbādā.
बिपिन गवन केवट अनुरागा । सुरसरि उतरि निवास प्रयागा ॥
bipina gavana kevaṭa anurāgā, surasari utari nivāsa prayāgā.

बालमीक प्रभु मिलन बखाना । चित्रकूट जिमि बसे भगवाना ॥
bālamīka prabhu milana bakhānā, citrakūṭa jimi base bhagavānā.
सचिवागवन नगर नृप मरना । भरतागवन प्रेम बहु बरना ॥
sacivāgavana nagara nṛpa maranā, bharatāgavana prema bahu baranā.
करि नृप क्रिया संग पुरबासी । भरत गए जहँ प्रभु सुख रासी ॥
kari nṛpa kriyā saṁga purabāsī, bharata gae jahaṁ prabhu sukha rāsī.
पुनि रघुपति बहुबिधि समुझाए । लै पादुका अवधपुर आए ॥
puni raghupati bahubidhi samujhāe, lai pādukā avadhapura āe.
भरत रहनि सुरपति सुत करनी । प्रभु अरु अत्रि भेंट पुनि बरनी ॥
bharata rahani surapati suta karanī, prabhu aru atri bheṁṭa puni baranī.

Trans:

Then came the narrative of Rāma's upcoming coronation, and of the king's vow and the sudden abdication of the royal state—and then, alas, the sorrow of the citizens at Shrī Rāma's parting! He next told of the colloquy between Rāma and Lakshman, the journey to the forest, the devotion of the boatman, the passage across the Gangā, and of the halt at Prayāg. He further described the Lord's meeting with Vālmikī and how the Lord-God, for some time, dwelt at Chitra-kūt. Next came the reaching of the minister to the city and the death of the king, and then the arrival of Bharat and the account of the abounding affection which Bharat had for Rāma. The crow further narrated how, after performing the king's obsequies, Bharat and the citizens betook themselves to their Lord—that Abode-of-Bliss; and how—after Rāma had said all he could to console them—Bharat returned to Awadh taking with him the Pādukā (wooden sandals) of Lord as his benefactor, guru, guide; and he further described Bharat's poignant mode of life. Next came the narration of the mischievous acts of the son of Indra, and the meeting of sage Atrī with the Lord.

दोहा-dohā:

कहि बिराध बध जेहि बिधि देह तजी सरभंग ।
kahi birādha badha jehi bidhi deha tajī sarabhaṁga.
बरनि सुतीछन प्रीति पुनि प्रभु अगस्ति सतसंग ॥ ६५ ॥
barani sutīchana prīti puni prabhu agasti satasaṁga. 65.

Trans:

Then Bhushuṁdi spoke of Viradh's death, and how Sarabhanga dropped his mortal coils, and of the devotion of Sutīkshan, and of the Lord's holy communion with sage Agastya.

चौपाई-caupāī:

कहि दंडक बन पावनताई । गीध मइत्री पुनि तेहिं गाई ॥
kahi daṁḍaka bana pāvanatāī, gīdha maitrī puni tehiṁ gāī.
पुनि प्रभु पंचबटीं कृत बासा । भंजी सकल मुनिन्ह की त्रासा ॥
puni prabhu paṁcabaṭīṁ kṛta bāsā, bhaṁjī sakala muninha kī trāsā.

पुनि लछिमन उपदेस अनूपा । सूपनखा जिमि कीन्हि कुरूपा ॥
puni lachimana upadesa anūpā, sūpanakhā jimi kīnhi kurūpā.
खर दूषन बध बहुरि बखाना । जिमि सब मरमु दसानन जाना ॥
khara dūṣana badha bahuri bakhānā, jimi saba maramu dasānana jānā.
दसकंधर मारीच बतकही । जेहि बिधि भई सो सब तेहिं कही ॥
dasakaṁdhara mārīca batakahī, jehi bidhi bhaī so saba tehiṁ kahī.
पुनि माया सीता कर हरना । श्रीरघुबीर बिरह कछु बरना ॥
puni māyā sītā kara haranā, śrīraghubīra biraha kachu baranā.
पुनि प्रभु गीध क्रिया जिमि कीन्ही । बधि कबंध सबरिहि गति दीन्ही ॥
puni prabhu gīdha kriyā jimi kīnhī, badhi kabaṁdha sabarihi gati dīnhī.
बहुरि बिरह बरनत रघुबीरा । जेहि बिधि गए सरोबर तीरा ॥
bahuri biraha baranata raghubīrā, jehi bidhi gae sarobara tīrā.

Trans:

He further recounted the chronicles of the purification of the Dandak forest by Shrī Rāma, and of the friendliness of the vulture, and of the Lord's stay in the woods of Panchvati, and how the Lord put an end to the fears of all the saints. Next came the incomparable discourse of the Lord which was made to Lakshman, and the story of Surpa-nakhā's mutilation, and the narrative of the death of Khar and Dūshan—and how Rāvan received the news and the particulars of his talk with Mārīch. Then came the abduction of the illusory Sītā, and a brief narration of Rāma's bereavement. After this the crow told how the Lord performed the vulture's funeral rites, how he slew Kabandh, and how he imparted salvation to Shabarī. Next was the episode of Raghubīr's desolation as he went to the shores of Lake Pampā.

दोहा-dohā:

प्रभु नारद संबाद कहि मारुति मिलन प्रसंग ।
prabhu nārada saṁbāda kahi māruti milana prasaṁga,
पुनि सुग्रीव मिताई बालि प्रान कर भंग ॥६६क॥
puni sugrīva mitāī bāli prāna kara bhaṁga. 66((ka).

कपिहि तिलक करि प्रभु कृत सैल प्रबरषन बास ।
kapihi tilaka kari prabhu kṛta saila prabaraṣana bāsa,
बरनन बर्षा सरद अरु राम रोष कपि त्रास ॥६६ख॥
baranana barṣā sarada aru rāma roṣa kapi trāsa. 66(kha).

Trans:

Now comes the dialogue between the Lord and Nārad and the account of the Lord's meeting with the son-of-wind, and of the Lord's alliance with Sugrīva, and of the drawing out of Vālī's life. Bhushuṁḍi continued with the account of the Lord making Sugrīva the king of monkeys, and then His taking up an abode on Mount-Prabarshan during the rains. He also described the seasons of rain and the autumn, and the wrath of Rāma upon Sugrīva, and the ensuing alarm of monkeys.

चौपाई-caupāī:

जेहि बिधि कपिपति कीस पठाए । सीता खोज सकल दिसि धाए ॥
jehi bidhi kapipati kīsa paṭhāe, sītā khoja sakala disi dhāe.
बिबर प्रबेस कीन्ह जेहि भाँती । कपिन्ह बहोरि मिला संपाती ॥
bibara prabesa kīnha jehi bhāṁtī, kapinha bahori milā saṁpātī.
सुनि सब कथा समीरकुमारा । नाघत भयउ पयोधि अपारा ॥
suni saba kathā samīrakumārā, nāghata bhayau payodhi apārā.
लंकाँ कपि प्रबेस जिमि कीन्हा । पुनि सीतहि धीरजु जिमि दीन्हा ॥
laṁkāṁ kapi prabesa jimi kīnhā, puni sītahi dhīraju jimi dīnhā.
बन उजारि रावनहि प्रबोधी । पुर दहि नाघेउ बहुरि पयोधी ॥
bana ujāri rāvanahi prabodhī, pura dahi nāgheu bahuri payodhī.
आए कपि सब जहँ रघुराई । बैदेही कि कुसल सुनाई ॥
āe kapi saba jahaṁ raghurāī, baidehī ki kusala sunāī.
सेन समेति जथा रघुबीरा । उतरे जाइ बारिनिधि तीरा ॥
sena sameti jathā raghubīrā, utare jāi bārinidhi tīrā.
मिला बिभीषन जेहि बिधि आई । सागर निग्रह कथा सुनाई ॥
milā bibhīṣana jehi bidhi āī, sāgara nigraha kathā sunāī.

Trans:

Next was the narrative of how the monkey-king dispatched his troops—who rushed in all directions to search for Sītā; and how during their search Hanumān and others entered a cave and found Sampātī. Now Hanumān—having heard from Sampātī of the whereabouts of Sītā—bounded over the mighty sea and made his way into Lankā, and there he brought comfort and solace to Sītā; and Hanumān then laid waste to the Ashoka-Grove, and admonished Rāvan, and further set ablaze the entire city of Lankā—before leaping back across the sea again. The narration continued with the monkeys all rejoining Rāma and telling him of the welfare of Sītā; how Raghubīr then, with his army, sallied forth to Lankā and encamped on the seashore; how Vibhīshan came to meet him; and how the ocean was subjugated.

दोहा-dohā:

सेतु बाँधि कपि सेन जिमि उतरी सागर पार ।
setu bāṁdhi kapi sena jimi utarī sāgara pāra,
गयउ बसीठी बीरबर जेहि बिधि बालिकुमार ॥ ६७क ॥
gayau basīṭhī bīrabara jehi bidhi bālikumāra. 67(ka).

निसिचर कीस लराई बरनिसि बिबिधि प्रकार ।
nisicara kīsa larāī baranisi bibidhi prakāra,
कुंभकरन घननाद कर बल पौरुष संघार ॥६७ख॥
kuṁbhakarana ghananāda kara bala pauruṣa saṁghāra. 67(kha).

Trans:

Bhushuṁḍi described how the bridge was built, and how the monkey hosts crossed over to the other side, and how Aṁgad, the valiant son of Vālī, went to Rāvan as an envoy. He further depicted the various battles between the demons and the monkeys, the might and valor of Kumbhkaran and Meghnād, and their eventual deaths in battle.

चौपाई-caupāī:

निसिचर निकर मरन बिधि नाना । रघुपति रावन समर बखाना ॥
nisicara nikara marana bidhi nānā, raghupati rāvana samara bakhānā.
रावन बध मंदोदरि सोका । राज बिभीषन देव असोका ॥
rāvana badha maṁdodari sokā, rāja bibhīṣana deva asokā.
सीता रघुपति मिलन बहोरी । सुरन्ह कीन्हि अस्तुति कर जोरी ॥
sītā raghupati milana bahorī, suranha kīnhi astuti kara jorī.
पुनि पुष्पक चढ़ि कपिन्ह समेता । अवध चले प्रभु कृपा निकेता ॥
puni puṣpaka caṛhi kapinha sametā, avadha cale prabhu kṛpā niketā.
जेहि बिधि राम नगर निज आए । बायस बिसद चरित सब गाए ॥
jehi bidhi rāma nagara nija āe, bāyasa bisada carita saba gāe.
कहेसि बहोरि राम अभिषेका । पुर बरनत नृपनीति अनेका ॥
kahesi bahori rāma abhiṣekā, pura baranata nṛpanīti anekā.
कथा समस्त भुसुंड बखानी । जो मैं तुम्ह सन कही भवानी ॥
kathā samasta bhusuṁḍa bakhānī, jo maiṁ tumha sana kahī bhavānī.
सुनि सब राम कथा खगनाहा । कहत बचन मन परम उछाहा ॥
suni saba rāma kathā khaganāhā, kahata bacana mana parama uchāhā.

Trans:

The chronicle continued with the deaths of all the different demons, the fight between Rāma and Rāvan, the death of Rāvan, and the mourning of Mandodarī. Next came the enthronement of Vibhīshan, the cessation of the sorrow of gods, and the reunion of Rāma and Sītā—and how the gods with clasped hands hymned their praises. Next the all-merciful Lord, along with the monkeys, mounted the aerial car Pushpak and set forth for Awadh. And thus Shrī Rāma finally arrived in his own Kingdom—all these glorious doings were sung by the crow; and then he told of Rāma's coronation and he described the city and all its sovereign polity. This entire history did Bhushuṁdi recount in detail, as I have told it to you, O Bhawānī. When the king of the birds had heard it all, his soul was in raptures and he spoke reverently:

सोरठा-soraṭhā:

गयउ मोर संदेह सुनेउँ सकल रघुपति चरित ।

gayau mora saṁdeha suneuṁ sakala raghupati carita,

भयउ राम पद नेह तव प्रसाद बायस तिलक ॥६८क॥

bhayau rāma pada neha tava prasāda bāyasa tilaka. 68(ka).

Trans:

"My doubts are all gone—now that I have heard the whole sanctifying history of Shrī Rāma. By your favor, O best of crows, I now feel great devotion to the hallowed feet of Shri Rāma, the Lord God."

इति श्रीमद्रामचरितमानसे सकलकलिकलुषविध्वंसने श्रीकाकभुसुंडिरामायण

iti śrīmadrāmacaritamānase sakalakalikaluṣavidhvaṁsane śrīkākabhusuṁḍirāmāyaṇa

---

Thus ends Śrī-Kākabhusuṁḍi-Rāmāyaṇa from Śrīmad-Rāmacaritamānas which eradicates all the impurities of the Kali-Yug

(Author of this Original Devanāgri Hymn is: Goswamī Tulsīdās [16th Century Saint]. Translator: Sushma)

सीताराम
सीताराम सीताराम
सीताराम सीताराम
सीताराम सीताराम

ॐ

श्री गणेशाय नमः
OM śrī gaṇeśāya namaḥ

श्रीजानकीवल्लभो विजयते
śrījānakīvallabho vijayate

श्रीनामरामायणम

śrī nāma rāmāyaṇam

सीताराम सीताराम सीताराम सीताराम सीताराम

—:—

-- बालकाण्डः -- bālakāṇḍaḥ --

॥ शुद्धब्रह्मपरात्पर राम ॥

śuddha-brahma-parāt-para rāma .1.
Behold Rāma—of the nature of pure Braham,
who is the Supreme-One, second to none.

॥ कालात्मकपरमेश्वर राम ॥

kāl-ātmaka-param-eśvara rāma .2.
Behold Rāma—Sovereign Godhead, the embodiment of Eternal Time.

॥ शेषतल्पसुखनिद्रित राम ॥

śeṣa-talpa-sukha-nidrita rāma .3.
Behold Rāma—who slumbers joyously on the bed made of
serpent Shesha Naga.

॥ ब्रह्माद्यमरप्रार्थित राम ॥

brahm-ādy-amara-prār-thita rāma .4.
Behold Rāma—whose Lotus Feet are venerated by Brahmmā and other
divinities—with a view to attaining ever-lasting life.

॥ चण्डकिरणकुलमण्डन राम ॥

caṇḍa-kiraṇa-kula-maṇḍana rāma .5.
Behold Rāma—the shining Jewel of the Solar-Dynasty.

॥ श्रीमद्दशरथनन्दन राम ॥

śrīmad-daśaratha-nandana rāma .6.
Behold Rāma—the illustrious Son of King Dashrath.

|| कौसल्यासुखवर्धन राम ||

kau-salyā-sukha-vardhana rāma .7.

Behold Rāma—who exceedingly amplifies His mother Kausalyā's joy.

|| विश्वामित्रप्रियधन राम ||

viśvā-mitra-priya-dhana rāma .8.

Behold Rāma—the very precious treasure of Sage Vishwāmitra.

|| घोरताटकाघातक राम ||

ghora-tāṭakā-ghātaka rāma .9.

Behold Rāma—Slayer of Tādaka, the terrible fiend.

|| मारीचादिनिपातक राम ||

mārīc-ādi-nipātaka rāma .10.

Behold Rāma—who wrought the downfall of Māricha and other Demons.

|| कौशिकमखसंरक्षक राम ||

kauśika-makha-saṁ-rakṣaka rāma .11.

Behold Rāma—the Guardian of the Yagya of Sage Vishwāmitra.

|| श्रीमदहल्योद्धारक राम ||

śrīmad-ahaly-oddhāraka rāma .12.

Behold Rāma—as He imparts redemption to the venerable Ahalyā.

|| गौतममुनिसंपूजित राम ||

gautama-muni-saṁ-pūjita rāma .13.

Behold Rāma—being worshipped by Muni Gautam.

|| सुरमुनिवरगणसंस्तुत राम ||

sura-muni-vara-gaṇa-saṁstuta rāma .14

Behold Rāma—who is ever praised by the gods and hosts of sages

|| नाविकधाविकमृदुपद राम ||

nāvika-dhāvika-mṛdu-pada rāma .15.

Behold Rāma—whose gentle feet are being washed by the Boatman.

|| मिथिलापुरजनमोहक राम ||

mithilā-pura-jana-mohaka rāma .16.

Behold Rāma—the Lordly prince who has so captivated the citizenry of Mithila.

|| विदेहमानसरञ्जक राम ||

videha-mānasa-rañjaka rāma .17.

Behold Rāma—who has enhanced the glory of King Janaka.

|| त्र्यंबककार्मुखभञ्जक राम ||

tryaṁbaka-kār-mukha-bhañjaka rāma .18.

Behold Rāma—as He breaks the Bow of the Three-Eyed Shiva.

|| सीतार्पितवरमालिक राम ||

sītār-pita-vara-mālika rāma .19.

Behold Sītā—who offers Her victory-garland to Rāma in matrimony.

|| कृतवैवाहिककौतुक राम ||

kṛta-vaivāhika-kautuka rāma .20.

Behold Rāma—as He enacts the sport of marriage ceremony.

|| भार्गवदर्पविनाशक राम ||

bhārgava-darpa-vināśaka rāma .21.

Behold Rāma—now seen destroying the pride of Parshurāma.

|| श्रीमदयोध्यापालक राम ||

śrīmad-ayodhyā-pālaka rāma .22.

Behold Rāma—the Lord-God, Ayodhya's Empyreal Sovereign.

राम राम जय राजा राम - राम राम जय सीता राम

rāma rāma jaya rājā rāma - rāma rāma jaya sītā rāma

Sing the glories of the Almighty—Raja Rāma; chant the Holy-Name Rāma-Rāma, Sītā-Rāma.

-- अयोध्याकाण्डः -- ayodhyākāṇḍaḥ --

|| अगणितगुणगणभूषित राम ||

agaṇita-guṇa-gaṇa-bhūṣita rāma .23.

Behold Rāma—who is graced with immeasurable virtues.

|| अवनीतनयाकामित राम ||

avanī-tanayā-kāmita rāma .24.

Behold Rāma—the heart's desire of Sītā: Daughter-of-the-Earth.

|| राकाचन्द्रसमानन राम ||

rākā-candra-samānana rāma .25.

Behold Rāma—whose resplendent face is like the full Moon.

|| पितृवाक्याश्रितकानन राम ||

pitṛ-vāky-āśrita-kānana rāma .26.

Behold Rāma—who leaves for exile to the forest
in order to honor His father's words.

|| प्रियगुहविनिवेदितपद राम ||

priya-guha-vinivedita-pada rāma .27.

Behold Rāma—unto whose holy feet Guha offers himself up as a cherished devotee.

|| तत्क्षालितनिजमृदुपद राम ||

tatkṣ-ālita-nija-mṛdu-pada rāma .28.

Behold Rāma—whose gentle feet Guha has the good fortune to lave.

|| भरद्वाजमुखानन्दक राम ||

bharadvāja-mukh-ānandaka rāma .29.

Behold Rāma—whose presence makes Sage Bharadwaja face lighten up with joy supreme.

|| चित्रकूटाद्रिनिकेतन राम ||

citrakūṭ-ādri-niketana rāma .30.

Behold Rāma—making Mount Chitrakut His habitat in the woods.

|| दशरथसन्ततचिन्तित राम ||

daśaratha-santata-cintita rāma .31.

Behold Rāma—ever mindful of Dashratha, His father, during the exile.

|| कैकेयीतनयार्थित राम ||

kaikeyī-tanay-ārthita rāma .32.

Behold Rāma—being eagerly besought by the son of Kaikayi to come return to His Kingdom.

|| विरचितनिजपितृकर्मक राम ||

vira-cita-nija-pitṛ-karmaka rāma .33.

Behold Rāma—seen performing the last rites of his sire—King Dashrath.

|| भरतार्पितनिजपादुक राम ||

bharat-ārpita-nija-pāduka rāma .34.

Behold Rāma—as He bestows His own Padukā to brother Bharat.

राम राम जय राजा राम - राम राम जय सीता राम

rāma rāma jaya rājā rāma - rāma rāma jaya sītā rāma

Sing the glories of the Almighty—Raja Rāma; chant the Holy-Name Rāma-Rāma, Sītā-Rāma.

-- अरण्यकाण्डः -- araṇyakāṇḍaḥ --

|| दण्डकावनजनपावन राम ||

daṇḍak-āvana-jana-pāvana rāma .35.

Behold Rāma—who has sanctified the Dandak Forest and the habitants therein.

॥ दुष्टविराधविनाशन राम ॥
duṣṭa-virādha-vināśana rāma .36.
Behold Rāma—who has destroyed Viradha the wicked demon.

॥ शरभङ्गसुतीक्ष्णार्चित राम ॥
śara-bhaṅga-sutīkṣṇ-ārcita rāma .37.
Behold Rāma—being worshipped by the sages Sharabhang and Sutīkshan.

॥ अगस्त्यानुग्रहवर्धित राम ॥
agasty-ānugraha-vardhita rāma .38.
Behold Rāma—augmented with the blessings and grace of sage Agastya.

॥ गृध्राधिपसंसेवित राम ॥
gṛdhr-ādhipa-saṁ-sevita rāma .39.
Behold Rāma—being honored by Jatāyu, the vulture-king.

॥ पञ्चवटीतटसुस्थित राम ॥
pañca-vaṭī-taṭa-susthita rāma .40.
Behold Rāma—dwelling on the banks of the river at Panchavati.

॥ शूर्पणखार्त्तिविधायक राम ॥.
śūrpa-ṇakh-ārtti-vidhāyaka rāma .41.
Behold Rāma—as He visits punishment upon Surpanakha for her wicked deeds.

॥ खरदूषणमुखसूदक राम ॥
khara-dūṣaṇa-mukha-sūdaka rāma .42.
Behold Rāma—seen effacing demons Khara and Dushana from the world.

॥ सीताप्रियहरिणानुग राम ॥
sītā-priya-hariṇ-ānuga rāma .43.
Behold Rāma—as He pursues the deer which Sītā has wished for herself.

॥ मारीचार्तिकृदाशुग राम ॥
mārīcārti-kṛdāśuga rāma .44.
Behold Rāma—who visits pain with an arrow upon Marich for his faults.

॥ विनष्टसीतान्वेषक राम ॥
vinaṣṭa-sītān-veṣaka rāma .45.
Behold Rāma—seen earnestly searching for Sītā, His beloved, who is found missing.

॥ गृध्राधिपगतिदायक राम ॥
gṛdhr-ādhipa-gati-dāyaka rāma .46.
Behold Rāma—imparting emancipation to Jatāyu, the vulture-king.

|| शबरीदत्तफलाशन राम ||

śabarī-datta-phalā-śana rāma .47.

Behold Rāma—partaking of the fruit offerings made by the woman sage Shabarī.

|| कबन्धबाहुच्छेदन राम ||

kabandha-bāhu-cchedana rāma .48.

Behold Rāma—severing the arms of Kabandh, the monster fiend.

राम राम जय राजा राम - राम राम जय सीता राम

rāma rāma jaya rājā rāma - rāma rāma jaya sītā rāma

Sing the glories of the Almighty—Raja Rāma; chant the Holy-Name Rāma-Rāma, Sītā-Rāma.

-- किष्किन्धाकाण्डः -- kiṣkindhākāṇḍaḥ --

|| हनुमत्सेवितनिजपद राम ||

hanumat-sevita-nija-pada rāma .49.

Behold Rāma—King of Kings, whose Holy Feet are being served by Hanumān, the monkey chief.

|| नतसुग्रीवाभीष्टद राम ||

nata-sugrīv-ābhīṣ-ṭada rāma .50.

Behold Rāma—granting the prayers of Sugrīva, who has arrived bowing to Him, seeking refuge.

|| गर्वितवालिसंहारक राम ||

garvita-vāli-saṁ-hāraka rāma .51.

Behold Rāma—who has put to death Vāli, the haughty monkey-king.

|| वानरदूतप्रेषक राम ||

vānara-dūta-preṣaka rāma .52.

Behold Rāma—who has sent monkeys as emissaries in search of Sītā.

|| हितकरलक्ष्मणसंयुत राम ||

hita-kara-lakṣmaṇa-saṁyuta rāma .53.

Behold Rāma—with Lakshman dwelling alongside Him, serving devotedly.

राम राम जय राजा राम - राम राम जय सीता राम

rāma rāma jaya rājā rāma - rāma rāma jaya sītā rāma

Sing the glories of the Almighty—Raja Rāma; chant the Holy-Name Rāma-Rāma, Sītā-Rāma.

॥ कपिवरसन्ततसंस्मृत राम ॥
kapi-vara-santata-saṁ-smṛta rāma .54.
Behold Rāma—who is continually thought upon by Hanumān, the most-excellent amongst the monkeys.

॥ तद्गतिविघ्नध्वंसक राम ॥
tad-gati-vighna-dhvaṁ-saka rāma .55.
Behold Rāma—as He removes all impediments & obstacles to the swiftness of Hanumān's rapid speed.

॥ सीताप्राणाधारक राम ॥
sītā-prāṇ-ādhāraka rāma .56.
Behold Rāma—the support and sustenance of the life of Sītā in captivity.

॥ दुष्टदशाननदूषित राम ॥
duṣṭa-daśānana-dūṣita rāma .57.
Behold Rāma—being affronted & marred by the wicked Ten-Headed Rāvan.

॥ शिष्टहनूमद्भूषित राम ॥
śiṣṭa-hanūmad-bhūṣita rāma .58.
Behold Rāma—praised & graced by the honorable Hanumān.

॥ सीतावेदितकाकावन राम ॥
sītā-vedita-kākā-vana rāma .59.
Behold Rāma—as He hears of the Kakasur incident in woods which was conveyed to Him by Shrī Sītā.

॥ कृतचूडामणिदर्शन राम ॥
kṛta-cūḍā-maṇi-darśana rāma .60.
Behold Rāma—beholding the head-crest chudāmani of Shrī Sītā.

॥ कपिवरवचनाश्वासित राम ॥
kapi-vara-vacan-āśvāsita rāma .61.
Behold Rāma—being comforted by the words of Shrī Hanumān, the wisest amongst the monkeys.

राम राम जय राजा राम - राम राम जय सीता राम
rāma rāma jaya rājā rāma - rāma rāma jaya sītā rāma
Sing the glories of the Almighty—Raja Rāma; chant the Holy-Name Rāma-Rāma, Sītā-Rāma.

-- युद्धकाण्डः -- yuddhakāṇḍaḥ --

|| रावणनिधनप्रस्थित राम ||

rāvaṇa-nidhana-prasthita rāma .62.

Behold Rāma—as He sallies forth to decimate Rāvan, the demon king.

|| वानरसैन्यसमावृत राम ||

vānara-sainya-sam-āvṛta rāma .63.

Behold Rāma—accompanied by the army of bears and monkeys.

|| शोषितसरिदीशार्थित राम ||

śoṣita-saridī-śārthita rāma .64.

Behold Rāma— being importuned by the king of oceans when He asks It to make way—and then makes ready to dry up the sea.

|| विभीष्णाभयदायक राम ||

vibhīṣṇ-ābhaya-dāyaka rāma .65.

Behold Rāma—who confers fearlessnes upon Vibhīshan who has come seeking sanctuary.

|| पर्वतसेतुनिबन्धक राम ||

parvata-setu-niban-dhaka rāma .66.

Behold Rāma—who has created a bridge of rocks across the ocean.

|| कुम्भकर्णशिरश्छेदक राम ||

kumbha karṇa śiraś chedaka rāma .67.

Behold Rāma— as He beheads Kumbhkaran in combat.

|| राक्षससङ्घविमर्दक राम राम ||

rākṣasa-saṅgha-vimardaka rāma .68.

Behold Rāma—crushing the army of demons on the battleground.

|| अहिमहिरावणचारण राम ||

ahi-mahi-rāvaṇa-cāraṇa rāma .69.

Behold Rāma—upon whom Ahi-Mahi Rāvana spied taking the guise of musician.

|| संहृतदशमुखरावण राम ||

saṁ-hṛta-daśa-mukha-rāvaṇa rāma .70.

Behold Rāma—as He kills the Ten-Headed Rāvan in the battle field.

|| विधिभवमुखसुरसंस्तुत राम ||

vidhi-bhava-mukha-sura-saṁ-stuta rāma .71

Behold Rāma—being worshiped by Brahmmā, Shiva and other Divinities.

॥ स्वस्थितदशरथवीक्षित राम ॥

svasthita-daśaratha-vīkṣita rāma .72.

Behold Rāma—whose divine deeds are being witnessed by father Dashratha from the Heavens.

॥ सीतादर्शनमोदित राम ॥

sītā-darśana-modita rāma .73.

Behold Rāma—as He beholds with delight Shrī Sītā after the battle is won.

॥ अभिषिक्तविभीषणनत राम ॥

abhi-ṣikta-vibhīṣaṇa-nata rāma .74.

Behold Rāma—being reverentially saluted by Vibhīshan after his own corronation.

॥ पुष्पकयानारोहण राम ॥

puṣpaka-yān-ārohaṇa rāma .75.

Behold Rāma—while He boards the aerial Pushpaka Vimana to return to Ayodhya His Kingdom.

॥ भरद्वाजादिनिषेवण राम ॥

bharadvāj-ādi-niṣevaṇa rāma .76.

Behold Rāma—being visited by sage Bharadwaja and the other sages.

॥ भरतप्राणप्रियकर राम ॥

bharata-prāṇa-priyakara rāma .77.

Behold Rāma—who brings joy to Bharta's life upon His return.

॥ साकेतपुरीभूषण राम ॥

sāketa-purī-bhūṣaṇa rāma .78.

Behold Rāma—the adornment of the city of Saket.

॥ सकलस्वीयसमानस राम ॥

sakala-svīya-sam-ānasa rāma .79.

Behold Rāma— being welcomed and venerated by the citizenry of Ayodhyā.

॥ रत्नलसत्पीठास्थित राम ॥

ratnal-asat-pīṭh-āsthita rāma .80.

Behold Rāma—seated on the Royal Throne embellished with shining jewels.

॥ पट्टाभिषेकालंकृत राम ॥

paṭṭ-ābhiṣek-ālaṁkṛta rāma .81.

Behold Rāma—adorned with the Royal Robes and Crown upon His coronation.

॥ पार्थिवकुलसम्मानित राम ॥

pārthiva-kula-sammānita rāma .82.

Behold Rāma—being honoured by the Assembly of Kings

॥ विभीषणार्पितरङ्गक राम ॥

vibhīṣaṇ-ārpita-raṅgaka rāma .83.

Behold Rāma—as He confers the idol of Shrī Ranganātha to Vibhishana.

॥ कीशकुलानुग्रहकर राम ॥

kīśa-kul-ānugraha-kara rāma .84.

Behold Rāma— showering His benediction upon the host of Monkeys.

॥ सकलजीवसंरक्षक राम ॥

sakala-jīva-saṁ-rakṣaka rāma .85.

Behold Rāma—the Guardian of all beings.

॥ समस्तलोकाधारक राम ॥

samasta-lokādhāraka-rāma .86.

Behold Rāma—the Sustainer of all the worlds.

राम राम जय राजा राम - राम राम जय सीता राम

rāma rāma jaya rājā rāma - rāma rāma jaya sītā rāma

Sing the glories of the Almighty—Raja Rāma; chant the Holy-Name Rāma-Rāma, Sītā-Rāma.

-- उत्तरकाण्डः -- uttarakāṇḍaḥ --

॥ आगत मुनिगण संस्तुत राम ॥

āgata muni-gaṇa saṁ-stuta rāma .87.

Behold Rāma—being revered by the visiting host of Munis.

॥ विश्रुतदशकण्ठोद्भव राम ॥

viśruta-daśa-kaṇṭh-odbhava rāma .88.

Behold Rāma—as He hears the story of origin of the Ten-Faced Rāvan.

॥ सितालिङ्गननिर्वृत राम ॥

sitā-liṅgana-nirvṛta rāma .89.

Behold Rāma—living happily, united with Sītā.

॥ नीतिसुरक्षितजनपद राम ॥

nīti-surakṣita-jana-pada rāma .90.

Behold Rāma—who protects His Sovereignity through Dharma—the moral-precept.

॥ विपिनत्याजितजनकज राम ॥
vipina-tyājita-janakaja rāma .91.
Behold Rāma—who has to abandon the daughter of Janak into the woods.

॥ कारितलवणासुरवध राम ॥
kārita-lavaṇāsura-vadha rāma .92.
Behold Rāma—as He brings about destruction of the Lavanasura Demon.

॥ स्वर्गतशम्बुक संस्तुत राम ॥
svargata-śambuka-saṁstuta rāma .93.
Behold Rāma—being praised by Shambuka, whom He sent to the Heavens.

॥ स्वतनयकुशलवनन्दित राम ॥
svatanaya-kuśa-lava-nandita rāma .94.
Behold Rāma—jubilant by the sight of His sons Kusha and Lava.

॥ अश्वमेधक्रतुदीक्षित राम ॥
aśva-medha-kratu-dīkṣita rāma .95.
Behold Rāma—performing the sacrifices of Ashwamedha Yagya, proper to a King.

॥ कालावेदितसुरपद राम ॥
kālā-vedita-sura-pada rāma .96.
Behold Rāma— as He is reminded of His Divine-Abode from Kāla, the mighty Time.

॥ आयोध्यकजनमुक्तित राम ॥
āyodhyaka-jana-muktita rāma .97.
Behold Rāma—conferring salvation upon all the inhabitants of Ayodhyā.

॥ विधिमुखविभुदानन्दक राम ॥
vidhi-mukha-vibhudā-nandaka rāma .98.
Behold Rāma—who causes the faces of Brahmmā and other gods to brighten up with joy.

॥ तेजोमयनिजरूपक राम ॥
tejo-maya-nija-rūpaka rāma .99.
Behold Rāma—who has assumed His own resplendent Divine-Form—fiery and gleaming.

॥ संसृतिबन्धविमोचक राम ॥
saṁsṛti-bandha-vimocaka rāma .100.
Behold Rāma—who releases one
from all the bondages of worldly existence.

॥ धर्मस्थापनतत्पर राम ॥

dharma-sthāpana-tatpara rāma .101.

Behold Rāma—ever ready to establish Dharma on Earth.

॥ भक्तिपरायणमुक्तिद् राम ॥

bhakti-parāyaṇa-muktida rāma .102.

Behold Rāma—giving salvation to Devotees that are completely dependent upon Him in thoughts, words, deeds.

॥ सर्वचराचरपालक राम ॥

sarva-carācara-pālaka rāma .103.

Behold Rāma—the Guardian of all beings, moving and non-moving.

॥ सर्वभवामयवारक राम ॥

sarva-bhavā-maya-vāraka rāma .104.

Behold Rāma—who takes His Devotees beyond the worldly dualities.

॥ वैकुण्ठालयसंस्थित राम ॥

vaikuṇṭh-ālaya-saṁ-sthita rāma .105.

Behold Rāma—ever established in His Divine Abode at Vaikuntha.

॥ नित्यानन्दपदस्थित राम ॥

nityā-nanda-pada-sthita rāma .106.

Behold Rāma—forever established as the Divine Godhead of Eternal Bliss.

॥ राम राम जय राजा राम ॥

rāma rāma jaya rājā rāma .107.

Sing the glories of the Almighty—Raja Rāma.

॥ राम राम जय सीता राम ॥

rāma rāma jaya sītā rāma .108.

Chant the Holy-Name Rāma-Rāma, glory to Sītā-Rāma.

राम राम जय राजा राम - राम राम जय सीता राम

rāma rāma jaya rājā rāma - rāma rāma jaya sītā rāma

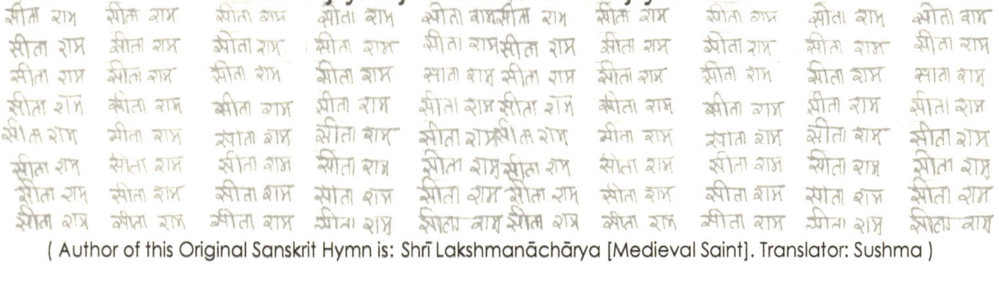

(Author of this Original Sanskrit Hymn is: Shrī Lakshmanāchārya [Medieval Saint]. Translator: Sushma)

ॐ

श्री गणेशाय नमः

OM śrī gaṇeśāya namaḥ

श्रीजानकीवल्लभो विजयते

śrījānakīvallabho vijayate

श्रीरामाष्टोत्तरशतनामस्तोत्रं

śrī-rām-āṣṭottara-śata-nāma-stotraṁ

सीताराम सीताराम सीताराम सीताराम सीताराम सीताराम

—— The 108 Auspicious Names of Shri Rāma ——

श्रीराघवं दशरथात्मजमप्रमेयं
śrī-rāghavaṁ daśarath-ātmajam-aprameyaṁ
सीतापतिं रघुकुलान्वयरत्नदीपम् ।
sītā-patiṁ raghu-kul-ānvaya-ratna-dīpam ,
आजानुबाहुमरविन्ददलायताक्षं
ājānu-bāhum-aravinda-dalāya-tākṣaṁ
रामं निशाचरविनाशकरं नमामि ॥
rāmaṁ niśācara-vināśa-karaṁ namāmi .

Bow I to Shrī-Rāma—son of Dasaratha, incomparable, the beloved consort of Sītā, the shining gem and leading light of the clan of Raghus—with long arms reaching upto His knees and eyes resembling petals of a lotus flower; unto Him Rāma, who is the annihilator of the night-wandering Rākshasas of the world, I offer salutations.

⌘

वैदेहीसहितं सुरद्रुमतले हैमे महामण्डपे
vaidehī-sahitaṁ sura-druma-tale haime mahā-maṇḍape
मध्ये पुष्पकमासने मणिमये वीरासने सुस्थितम् ।
madhye puṣpakam-āsane maṇi-maye vīr-āsane su-sthitam ,
अग्रे वाचयति प्रभञ्जनसुते तत्त्वं मुनिभ्यः परं
agre vāca-yati pra-bhañjana-sute tattvaṁ muni-bhyaḥ paraṁ
व्याख्यान्तं भरतादिभिः परिवृतं रामं भजे श्यामलम् ॥
vyākhy-āntaṁ bharat-ādibhiḥ pari-vṛtaṁ rāmaṁ bhaje śyāmalam .

I bow to Lord Rāma who—along with His beloved consort Sītā, daughter of Videha—is seated under the shade of Kalpavriksha (the Divine Wish-Tree) nestled in a grand gilded altar, set within the middle of the aerial Pushpaka Vimāna—upon a splendid throne constellated with gems. Encircled by brothers Bharatha and others, Rāma sits—well settled, sporting the posture of the bravest hero—while in front abides the son of Prabhanjana (Hanumān) standing in veneration, enunciating the grand maxim: that Rāma is the Supreme Truth sung of and extolled by sages.

⌘

श्रीरामो रामभद्रश्च रामचन्द्रश्च शाश्वतः ।
śrīrāmo rāma-bhadra-śca rāma-candra-śca śāśvataḥ ,
राजीवलोचनः श्रीमान् राजेन्द्रो रघुपुङ्गवः ॥ १ ॥
rājīva-locanaḥ śrīmān rājendro raghu-puṅgavaḥ .1.

Glory be to Shrī Rāma, Bestower of Felicity, the all-auspicious Lord, shining like the full-moon, the eternal Divine-Being of lotus-eyes, abode of Laxmi, King-of-Kings, the grandest Scion of the Dynasty of Raghus.

⌘

जानकीवल्लभो जैत्रो जितामित्रो जनार्दनः ।
jānakī-vallabho jaitro jitā-mitro jan-ārdanaḥ ,
विश्वामित्रप्रियो दान्तः शरणत्राणतत्परायः ॥ २ ॥
viśvā-mitra-priyo dāntaḥ śaraṇa-trāṇa-tatparāyḥ .2.

Glory be to the Beloved of Jānakī, the ever-victorious, vanquisher of foes, the redeemer of beings, dearest disciple of Vishwāmitra, self-disciplined, ever determined to protect those who take refuge in Him.

⌘

वालिप्रमथनो वाग्मी सत्यवाक् सत्यविक्रमः ।
vāli-pra-mathano vāgmī satyavāk satya-vikramaḥ ,
सत्यव्रतो व्रतधरः सदा हनुमदाश्रितः ॥ ३ ॥
satya-vrato vrata-dharaḥ sadā hanumad-āśritaḥ .3.

Glory be to the Victor of Vāli, the Eloquent One, of Truthful speech, valiant in defending the Truth—of truthful Vows, practician of penance, the Lord-God ever served under the aegis of Shrī Hanumān.

⌘

कौसलेयः खरध्वंसी विराधवधपण्डितः ।
kausal-eyaḥ khara-dhvaṁsī virādha-vadha-paṇḍitaḥ ,

विभीषणपरित्राता हरकोदण्डखण्डनः ॥ ४ ॥
vibhīṣaṇa-pari-trātā hara-kodaṇḍa-khaṇḍanaḥ .4.

Glory be to Kausalyā's son, Destroyer of the demon Khara, skillful in subjugating the monster Virādha, the Protector of Vibhishan—the One who broke the mighty Bow of Shiva.

⌘

सप्ततालप्रभेत्ता च दशग्रीवशिरोहरः ।
sapta-tāla-pra-bhettā ca daśa-grīva-śiro-haraḥ ,
जामदग्न्यमहादर्पदलनस्ताटकान्तकः ॥ ५ ॥
jāma-dagnya-mahā-darpa-dalanas-tāṭak-āntakaḥ .5.

Glory be to the Valorous Rāma who pierced the seven Tāla Trees with a single arrow, who cut off the ten-heads of Rāvan, who shattered the inordinate arrogance of Jamadagni's son, and who slew Tāṭakā the terrible demon.

⌘

वेदान्तसारो वेदात्मा भवरोगस्य भेषजम् ।
vedānta-sāro ved-ātmā bhava-rogasya bheṣajam ,
दूषणत्रिशिरो हन्ता त्रिमूर्तिस्त्रिगुणात्मकः ॥ ६ ॥
dūṣaṇa-tri-śiro hantā tri-mūrtis-triguṇ-ātmakaḥ .6.

Glory be to Rāma, the Essence of Vedānta, the Personification of the Vedas, Reliever of all earthly ailments, the slayer of monsters Dūṣaṇa & Triśira, the Lord-God manifest as the Trinity of Brahmmā, Vishnu, Mahesh—and from whom emanate the three gunas of Māyā.

त्रिविक्रमस्त्रिलोकात्मा पुण्यचारित्रकीर्तनः ।
tri-vikramas-trilok-ātmā puṇya-cāritra-kīrtanaḥ ,
त्रिलोकरक्षको धन्वी दण्डकारण्यपावनः ॥ ७ ॥
tri-loka-rakṣako dhanvī daṇḍak-āraṇya-pāvanaḥ .7.

Glory be to the Lord who spanned the Three-Regions of the Universe with His feet, the Lord-God pervaded throughout earth, hell and heaven, whose hallowed deeds are sung through Hymns, who's the Protector of the Three-Worlds, the Wielder of the Bow, and who sanctifed the Dandaka forest by dwelling there.

⌘

अहल्याशापशमनः पितृभक्तो वरप्रदः ।
ahalyā-śāpa-śamanaḥ pitṛ-bhakto vara-pradaḥ ,
जितेन्द्रियो जितक्रोधो जितामित्रो जगद्गुरुः ॥ ८ ॥
jit-endriyo jita-krodho jitā-mitro jagad-guruḥ .8.

Glory be to Shrī-Rāma, the Remover of Ahalyā's curse, ever devoted to His father Dashrath, the Conferrer of boons, Conqueror of sense-organs, the Victor over anger, who wins over friends—and who is the supreme Guru of the whole world.

⌘

ऋक्षवानरसंघाती चित्रकूटसमाश्रयः ।
ṛkṣa-vānara-saṁghātī citra-kūṭa-sam-āśrayaḥ ,
जयन्तत्राणवरदः सुमित्रापुत्रसेवितः ॥ ९ ॥
jayanta-trāṇa-varadaḥ sumitrā-putra-sevitaḥ .9.

Glory be to Shrī-Rāma—the Lord who presided over the hosts of bears and monkeys, who dwelt at the Chitrakūta Hill, who saved Jayanta—the Lord-God ever served by Sumitrā's son Lakshman.

⌘

सर्वदेवादिदेवश्च मृतवानरजीवनः ।
sarva-dev-ādi-deva-śca mṛta-vānara-jīvanaḥ ,
मायामारीचहन्ता च महादेवो महाभुजः ॥ १० ॥
māyā-mārīca-hantā ca mahā-devo mahā-bhujaḥ .10.

Glory be to the God of gods Rāma—the Lord who revived the dead monkeys, the slayer of Maricha, the illusion practicing demon—the Greatest-God of mighty arms.

⌘

सर्वदेवस्तुतः सौम्यो ब्रह्मण्यो मुनिसंस्तुतः ।
sarva-deva-stutaḥ saumyo brahm-aṇyo muni-saṁ-stutaḥ ,
महायोगी महोदारः सुग्रीवेप्सितराज्यदः ॥ ११ ॥
mahā-yogī maho-dāraḥ sugrī-vepsita-rājyadaḥ .11.

Glory be to Shrī Rāma, the God praised by all Divinities, the Ocean of Tranqiility, the Absolute Reality, who is worshipped by hosts of Munis, the Great Yogī, the Noble-Most, the Lord who bestowed the kingdom of Kishkindhā upon Sugrīva.

⌘

सर्वपुण्याधिकफलः स्मृतसर्वाघनाशनः ।
sarva-puṇy-ādhika-phalaḥ smṛta-sarvā-ghanā-śanaḥ ,
आदिदेवो महादेवो महापूरुष एव च ॥ १२ ॥
ādi-devo mahā-devo mahā-pūruṣa eva ca .12.

Glory be to Shrī-Rāma, yield of meritorious acts, the Remover of afflictions—the Primordial Entity, the Highest God, the Supreme Being.

⌘

पुण्योदयो दयासारः पुराणपुरुषोत्तमः ।
puṇyo-dayo dayā-sāraḥ purāṇa-puruṣ-ottamaḥ ,
स्मितवक्त्रो मिताभाषी पूर्वभाषी च राघवः ॥ १३ ॥
smita-vaktro mitā-bhāṣī pūrva-bhāṣī ca rāghavaḥ .13.

Glory be to Shrī-Rāma, the source of every blessing & good furtune, the embodiment of compassion, the Supreme whose laurels are sung in the Purānas—the Lord who speaks smilingly, is reticent and mellifluent, who can speak of things to come, the brightest scion of the Raghu dynasty.

⌘

अनन्तगुणगम्भीरो धीरोदात्तगुणोत्तमः ।
ananta-guṇa-gambhīro dhīro-dātta-guṇ-ottamaḥ ,
मायामानुषचारित्रो महादेवादिपूजितः ॥ १४ ॥
māyā-mānuṣa-cāritro mahā-dev-ādi-pūjitaḥ .14.

Glory be to Shrī-Rāma, the majestic Lord of infinite qualities, conferer of courage and superlative virtues, the God who became Incarnate presiding over Māyā—the Lord-God worshiped by God of gods Shiva & other divinities.

⌘

सेतुकृज्जितवारीशः सर्वतीर्थमयो हरिः ।
setu-kṛ-jjita-vārīśaḥ sarva-tīrtha-mayo hariḥ ,
श्यामाङ्गः सुन्दरः शूरः पीतवासा धनुर्धरः ॥ १५ ॥
śyām-āṅgaḥ sundaraḥ śūraḥ pīta-vāsā dhanur-dharaḥ .15.

Glory be to Shrī-Rāma who created the bridge across the ocean, the Conqueror of desires, the God who is the sum of all Holy Places, the Lord-God Uprooter of sins, the Dark-Complexioned, most Beautiful & Valiant Lord donned in yellow apparels wielding the Bow.

⌘

सर्वयज्ञाधिपो यज्वा जरामरणवर्जितः ।

sarva-yajñ-ādhipo yajvā jarā-maraṇa-varjitaḥ ,

शिवलिङ्गप्रतिष्ठाता सर्वावगुणवर्जितः ॥ १६ ॥

śiva-liṅga-pratiṣṭh-ātā sarvāva-guṇa-varjitaḥ .16.

Glory be to Shrī-Rāma, the Lord of sacrifices, the Sacrificer, He who is beyond age & death, He who installed the Shivalingam at Rāmeshwaram, the Lord bereft of evil.

⌘

परमात्मा परं ब्रह्म सच्चिदानन्दविग्रहः ।

param-ātmā paraṁ brahma sac-cid-ānanda-vigrahaḥ ,

परं ज्योतिः परंधाम पराकाशः परात्परः ॥ १७ ॥

paraṁ jyotiḥ paraṁ-dhāma parā-kāśaḥ parā-tparaḥ .17.

Glory be to Shrī-Rāma, the Soul of Souls, the Supreme Absolute, the embodied Super-Consciosuness of the nature of Existence,-Knowledge-Bliss; the Fiery Light, the Final Abode, the Sovereign Space—the Highest amongst the Highest.

⌘

परेशः पारगः पारः सर्वदेवात्मकः परः ॥

pareśaḥ pāragaḥ pāraḥ sarva-devātmakaḥ paraḥ .

Glory be to the Supreme Godhead, the Lord who takes His Devotees across the sea of births and deaths, the Transcendent Being, the Self of all gods: our Sovereign Lord-God Shrī-Rāma.

⌘

॥ इति श्रीरामाष्टोत्तरशतनामस्तोत्रं सम्पूर्णम् ॥

. iti śrīrāmāṣṭottaraśatanāmastotraṁ sampūrṇam .

— Thus ends Śrī-Rāmāṣṭottara-Śatanāma-Stotraṁ - the 108 names of the Lord —

(Author of this Original Sanskrit Hymn is: Shrī Vyāsa-Deva [Pre-historic Sage]. Translator: Sushma)

सीताराम
सीताराम सीताराम
सीताराम सीताराम
सीताराम सीताराम

ॐ

श्री गणेशाय नमः
OM śrī gaṇeśāya namaḥ
श्रीजानकीवल्लभो विजयते
śrījānakīvallabho vijayate
श्रीरामाष्टोत्तरशतनामावलिः
śrī-rām-āṣṭottara-śata-nāmā-valiḥ

सीताराम सीताराम सीताराम सीताराम सीताराम सीताराम

The 108 Auspicious Names of Shri Rāma in List Form

1	ॐ श्रीरामाय नमः om śrī-rāmāya namaḥ	— my obeisance to — Śrī-Rāma – Giver of Happiness
2	ॐ रामभद्राय नमः Om rāma-bhadrāya namaḥ	— my obeisance to — Rāmabhadra – the All-Auspicious
3	ॐ रामचन्द्राय नमः om rāma-candrāya namaḥ	— my obeisance to — Rāmacandra – Alike the Lustrous Moon: charming & tranquil
4	ॐ शाश्वताय नमः om śāśvat-āya namaḥ	— my obeisance to — Śāśvata – the Eternal God
5	ॐ राजीवलोचनाय नमः om rājīva-locan-āya namaḥ	— my obeisance to — Rājīvalocana – the Lotus-Eyed
6	ॐ श्रीमते नमः om śrī-mate namaḥ	— my obeisance to — Śrīman – the Lord of Prosperity
7	ॐ राजेन्द्राय नमः om rāj-endrāya namaḥ	— my obeisance to — Rājendra – the King of Kings
8	ॐ रघुपुङ्गवाय नमः om raghu-puṅgav-āya namaḥ	— my obeisance to — Raghupuṅgava – the Most-Exalted Scion of Raghu-Dynasty
9	ॐ जानकीवल्लभाय नमः om jānakī-vallabh-āya namaḥ	— my obeisance to — Jānakīvallabha – the Beloved Consort of Jānakī
10	ॐ जैत्राय नमः om jaitr-āya namaḥ	— my obeisance to — Jaitra – the Triumphant One

11	ॐ जितामित्राय नमः om jitā-mitr-āya namaḥ	— my obeisance to — Jitāmitra – Vanquisher of foes
12	ॐ जनार्दनाय नमः om jan-ārdan-āya namaḥ	— my obeisance to — Janārdana – the Sustainer of all beings
13	ॐ विश्वामित्रप्रियाय नमः om viśvā-mitra-priy-āya namaḥ	— my obeisance to — Viśvāmitrapriya –the beloved pupil of Sage Vishwāmitra
14	ॐ दान्ताय नमः Om dānt-āya namaḥ	— my obeisance to — Dānta – Self-controlled
15	ॐ शरणत्राणतत्पराय नमः om śaraṇa-trāṇa-tatpar-āya namaḥ	— my obeisance to — Śaraṇatrāṇatatpara – Ever protective of His Devotees
16	ॐ वालिप्रमथनाय नमः om vāli-pramathan-āya namaḥ	— my obeisance to — Vālipramathana – Vanquisher of Vāli
17	ॐ वाग्मिने नमः om vāg-mine namaḥ	— my obeisance to — Vāgmine – Eloquent
18	ॐ सत्यवाचे नमः om satya-vāce namaḥ	— my obeisance to — Satyavāk – who speaks truthfully
19	ॐ सत्यविक्रमाय नमः om satya-vikram-āya namaḥ	— my obeisance to — Satyavikrama – Valiant in defending the Truth
20	ॐ सत्यव्रताय नमः om satya-vrat-āya namaḥ	— my obeisance to — Satyavrata – Pledged to uphold Veracity
21	ॐ व्रतधराय नमः om vrata-dhar-āya namaḥ	— my obeisance to — Vratadhara – the Keeper of Penance & Vows
22	ॐ सदाहनुमदाश्रिताय नमः om sadā-hanumad-āśrit-āya namaḥ	— my obeisance to — Sadāhanumadāśrita – Hanumān's eternal sanctuary
23	ॐ कौसलेयाय नमः om kausale-yāya namaḥ	— my obeisance to — Kausaleyā – Kausalyā's son
24	ॐ खरध्वंसिने नमः om khara-dhvaṁs-ine namaḥ	— my obeisance to — Kharadhvaṁsī – the Slayer of Demon Khara

25	ॐ विराधवधपंडिताय नमः om virādha-vadha-paṁḍit-āya namaḥ	— my obeisance to — Virādhavadhapaṇḍita – the masterly Destroyer of demon Virādha
26	ॐ विभीषणपरित्रात्रे नमः om vibhīṣaṇa-paritr-ātre namaḥ	— my obeisance to — Vibhīṣaṇaparitrātā – Protector of Vibhishan
27	ॐ हरकोदण्डखण्डनाय नमः om hara-kodaṇḍa-khaṇḍan-āya namaḥ	— my obeisance to — Harakodaṇḍakhaṇḍana – One who broke the mighty Bow-of-Shiva
28	ॐ सप्ततालप्रभेत्रे नमः om sapta-tāla-prabhetre namaḥ	— my obeisance to — Saptatālaprabhettā – He who pierced the seven Tāla trees with a single arrow
29	ॐ दशग्रीवशिरोहराय नमः om daśa-grīva-śiro-har-āya namaḥ	— my obeisance to — Daśagrīvaśirohara – Slayer of the Ten-Headed Rāvan
30	ॐ जामदग्न्यमहादर्पदलनाय नमः om jāma-dagnya-mahā-darpa-dalan-āya namaḥ	— my obeisance to — Jāmadagnyamahādarpadalana – He who shattered Parasurama's overabundant arrogance
31	ॐ ताटकान्तकाय नमः om tāṭakā-antak-āya namaḥ	— my obeisance to — Tāṭakāntaka – the Slayer of demon Tāṭaka
32	ॐ वेदान्तसाराय नमः om vedānta-sār-āya namaḥ	— my obeisance to — Vedāntasāra – the Essence of Vedanta
33	ॐ वेदात्मने नमः om ved-ātmane namaḥ	— my obeisance to — Vedātmā – Heart and soul of the Vedas
34	ॐ भवरोगस्य भेषजाय नमः om bhava-rogasya bheṣaj-āya namaḥ	— my obeisance to — Bhavarogasyabheṣajam – Reliever of every worldly ailment
35	ॐ दूषणत्रिशिरोहन्त्रे नमः om dūṣaṇa-triśiro-hantre namaḥ	— my obeisance to — Duṣaṇatriśirohantā – Slayer of Demons Dūṣaṇa & Triśira
36	ॐ त्रिमूर्तये नमः om tri-mūrt-aye namaḥ	— my obeisance to — Trimūrti – the Lord manifest in Triune Form: Brahmmā, Vishnu, Mahesh
37	ॐ त्रिगुणात्मकाय नमः om triguṇ-ātmak-āya namaḥ	— my obeisance to — Triguṇātmaka – from whom Māyā's Three Natures originate
38	ॐ त्रिविक्रमाय नमः om tri-vikram-āya namaḥ	— my obeisance to — Trivikrama – Lord of the Three-Worlds

39	ॐ त्रिलोकात्मने नमः om trilok-ātmane namaḥ	— my obeisance to — Trilokātmā – Supreme Soul of Three-Spheres.
40	ॐ पुण्यचारित्रकीर्तनाय नमः om puṇya-cāritra-kīrtan-āya namaḥ	— my obeisance to — Puṇyacāritrakīrtana – whose Holy-Enactments are sung all over through Hymns
41	ॐ त्रिलोकरक्षकाय नमः om triloka-rakṣak-āya namaḥ	— my obeisance to — Trilokarakṣaka – Protector of the Three-Worlds
42	ॐ धन्विने नमः om dhan-vine namaḥ	— my obeisance to — Dhanvī – Wielder of the Bow
43	ॐ दंडकारण्यवर्तनाय नमः om daṁḍak-āraṇya-vartan-āya namaḥ	— my obeisance to — Daṇḍakāraṇyavartana – He who sanctified the Dandaka forest by dwelling there
44	ॐ अहल्याशापविमोचनाय नमः om ahalyā-śāpa-vimocan-āya namaḥ	— my obeisance to — Ahalyāśāpaśamana – Remover of Ahalyā's curse
45	ॐ पितृभक्ताय नमः om pitṛ-bhakt-āya namaḥ	— my obeisance to — Pitṛbhakta – who was devoted to His father Dashrath
46	ॐ वरप्रदाय नमः om vara-pradāya namaḥ	— my obeisance to — Varaprada – Bestower of Boons
47	ॐ जितेन्द्रियाय नमः om jit-endriy-āya namaḥ	— my obeisance to — Jitendriya – Master of the Senses
48	ॐ जितक्रोधाय नमः om jita-krodh-āya namaḥ	— my obeisance to — Jitakrodha – Conqueror over Anger
49	ॐ जितमित्राय नमः om jita-mitr-āya namaḥ	— my obeisance to — Jitamitra – who wins over friends
50	ॐ जगद्गुरवे नमः om jagad-gurave namaḥ	— my obeisance to — Jagadguru – Supreme Guru of the world
51	ॐ ऋक्षवानरसङ्घातिने नमः om ṛkṣa-vānara-saṅghātine namaḥ	— my obeisance to — Ṛkṣavānarasaṅghātī – He who presided over legions of Bears & Monkeys
52	ॐ चित्रकूटसमाश्रयाय नमः om citra-kūṭa-sam-āśra-yāya namaḥ	— my obeisance to — Citrakūṭasamāśraya – the Lord who dwelt at Chitrakūt

53	ॐ जयन्तत्राणवरदाय नमः om jayanta-trāṇa-vara-dāya namaḥ	— my obeisance to — Jayantatrāṇavarada – the Boon Provider to save Jayant
54	ॐ सुमित्रापुत्रसेविताय नमः om sumitrā-putra-sevit-āya namaḥ	— my obeisance to — Sumitrāputrasevita – the Lord ever served by Sumitrā's son: Lakshman
55	ॐ सर्वदेवादिदेवाय नमः om sarva-devādi-dev-āya namaḥ	— my obeisance to — Sarvadevādideva – the Lord over all gods and divinities
56	ॐ मृतवानरजीवनाय नमः om mṛta-vānara-jīvan-āya namaḥ	— my obeisance to — Mṛtavānarajīvana – the Resurrecter of dead monkeys
57	ॐ मायामारीचहन्त्रे नमः om māyā-mārīca-hantre namaḥ	— my obeisance to — Māyāmārīcahantā – Destroyer of Māricha, the illusory demon
58	ॐ महादेवाय नमः om mahā-dev-āya namaḥ	— my obeisance to — Mahādeva – the Great God
59	ॐ महाभुजाय नमः om mahā-bhuj-āya namaḥ	— my obeisance to — Mahābhuja – the Lord of mighty arms
60	ॐ सर्वदेवस्तुताय नमः om sarva-deva-stut-āya namaḥ	— my obeisance to — Sarvadevastuta – Lord-God praised by all Divinities
61	ॐ सौम्याय नमः om saum-yāya namaḥ	— my obeisance to — Saumya – the Benevolent Lord, of calm demeanor
62	ॐ ब्रह्मण्याय नमः om brahmaṇ-yāya namaḥ	— my obeisance to — Brahmaṇya – the Absolute Reality
63	ॐ मुनिसंस्तुताय नमः om muni-saṁ-stut-āya namaḥ	— my obeisance to — Munisaṁstuta – the Lord-God worshipped by Saints
64	ॐ महायोगिने नमः om mahā-yogine namaḥ	— my obeisance to — Mahāyogī – the greatest of Yogīs
65	ॐ महोदराय नमः om maho-dar-āya namaḥ	— my obeisance to — Mahodara – the most Noble
66	ॐ सुग्रीवेप्सितराज्यदाय नमः om sugrīv-epsita-rājya-dāya namaḥ	— my obeisance to — Sugrīvepsitarājyada – the Lord who bestowed kingdom upon Sugrīva

67	ॐ सर्वपुण्याधिकफलाय नमः om sarva-puṇy-ādhika-phal-āya namaḥ	— my obeisance to — Sarvapuṇyādhikaphala – Yield of meritorious deeds & virtues
68	ॐ स्मृतसर्वौघनाशनाय नमः om smṛta-sarv-augha-nāśan-āya namaḥ	— my obeisance to — Smṛtasarvāghanāśana – Remover of all afflictions
69	ॐ आदिपुरुषाय नमः om ādi-puruṣ-āya namaḥ	— my obeisance to — Ādipuruṣa – the Primordial Entity
70	ॐ परमपुरुषाय नमः om parama-puruṣ-āya namaḥ	— my obeisance to — Paramapuruṣa – the Highest Existence
71	ॐ महापुरुषाय नमः om mahā-puruṣ-āya namaḥ	— my obeisance to — Mahāpuruṣa – the Great Being
72	ॐ पुण्योदयाय नमः om puṇy-oday-āya namaḥ	— my obeisance to — Puṇyodaya – Source of every blessing & good fortune
73	ॐ दयासाराय नमः om dayā-sār-āya namaḥ	— my obeisance to — Dayāsāra – Personification of kindness and compassion
74	ॐ पुराणपुरुषोत्तमाय नमः om purāṇa-puruṣ-ottam-āya namaḥ	— my obeisance to — Purāṇapuruṣottama – the Supreme Being whose laurels are sung in the Purānas
75	ॐ स्मितवक्त्राय नमः om smita-vaktr-āya namaḥ	— my obeisance to — Smitavaktra – the Lord of smiling face
76	ॐ मितभाषिणे नमः om mita-bhāṣ-iṇe namaḥ	— my obeisance to — Mitabhāṣī – the Reticent One, of mellifluent speech
77	ॐ पूर्वभाषिणे नमः om pūrva-bhāṣ-iṇe namaḥ	— my obeisance to — Pūrvabhāṣī – who speaks before
78	ॐ राघवाय नमः om rāghav-āya namaḥ	— my obeisance to — Rāghava – Scion of the Raghu-Dynasty
79	ॐ अनन्तगुणगम्भीराय नमः om ananta-guṇa-gambhīr-āya namaḥ	— my obeisance to — Anantaguṇagambhīra – Lord of infinite eminent virtues
80	ॐ धीरोदात्तगुणोत्तमाय नमः om dhīro-dātta-guṇ-ottam-āya namaḥ	— my obeisance to — Dhīrodāttaguṇottama – Wielding Steadiness, highest virtue

81	ॐ मायामानुषचारित्राय नमः om māyā-mānuṣa-cāritr-āya namaḥ	— my obeisance to — Māyāmānuṣacāritra – the Lord, who presiding over Māyā, became Incarnate in human form
82	ॐ महादेवादिपूजिताय नमः om mahā-devādi-pūjit-āya namaḥ	— my obeisance to — Mahādevādipūjita – the Lord-God worshipped by Lord Shiva & other Divinities
83	ॐ सेतुकृते नमः om setu-kṛte namaḥ	— my obeisance to — Setukṛte – Builder of Bridge
84	ॐ जितवाराशये नमः om jita-vār-āśaye namaḥ	— my obeisance to — Jitavārāśaya – Conqueror over Desires
85	ॐ सर्वतीर्थमयाय नमः om sarva-tīrthama-yāya namaḥ	— my obeisance to — Sarvatīrthamaya – the sum of all Holy Pilgrimages
86	ॐ हरये नमः om har-aye namaḥ	— my obeisance to — Hari – Supreme Lord-God, Destroyer of Sin
87	ॐ श्यामाङ्गाय नमः om śyām-āṅg-āya namaḥ	— my obeisance to — Śyāmāṅga – the Dark-Complexioned God
88	ॐ सुन्दराय नमः om sundar-āya namaḥ	— my obeisance to — Sundara – Most-Beautiful One
89	ॐ शूराय नमः om śūr-āya namaḥ	— my obeisance to — Śūra – Valiant & Valorous
90	ॐ पीतवाससे नमः om pīta-vās-ase namaḥ	— my obeisance to — Pītavāsa – the Lord dressed in beautiful yellow apparels
91	ॐ धनुर्धराय नमः om dhanur-dhar-āya namaḥ	— my obeisance to — Dhanurdhara – Bearer of the Bow
92	ॐ सर्वयज्ञाधिपाय नमः om sarva-yajñ-ādhip-āya namaḥ	— my obeisance to — Sarvayajñādhipa – Lord of all Sacrifices
93	ॐ यज्विने नमः om yajvine namaḥ	— my obeisance to — Yajvine – Performer of great Yajnas
94	ॐ जरामरणवर्जिताय नमः om jarā-maraṇa-varjit-āya namaḥ	— my obeisance to — Jarāmaraṇavarjita – upon whom Death & Ageing never comes

95	ॐ शिवलिङ्गप्रतिष्ठात्रे नमः om śiva-liṅga-pra-tiṣṭh-ātre namaḥ	— my obeisance to — Śivaliṅgapratiṣṭhātre – He who installed the Shiva-Linga
96	ॐ सर्वावगुणवर्जिताय नमः om sarv-āvaguṇa-varjit-āya namaḥ	— my obeisance to — Sarvāvaguṇavarjita – in whom is no evil quality
97	ॐ परमात्मने नमः om param-ātm-ane namaḥ	— my obeisance to — Paramātma– All-Pervading Soul of Souls
98	ॐ परब्रह्मणे नमः om para-brahm-aṇe namaḥ	— my obeisance to — Parabrahma – the Absolute-Reality
99	ॐ सच्चिदानन्दविग्रहाय नमः om sac-cid-ānanda-vigrah-āya namaḥ	— my obeisance to — Saccidānandavigraha – Embodiment of Consciousness: of the nature of Existence-Knowledge-Bliss
100	ॐ परञ्ज्योतिषे नमः om parañ-jyoti-ṣe namaḥ	— my obeisance to — Paraṁjyoti – Supreme Self-Effulgent Light
101	ॐ परन्धाम्ने नमः om paran-dhām-ne namaḥ	— my obeisance to — Paraṁdhāma – the Supreme Abode
102	ॐ पराकाशाय नमः om parā-kāś-āya namaḥ	— my obeisance to — Parākāśa – Supreme Space
103	ॐ परात्पराय नमः om parāt-par-āya namaḥ	— my obeisance to — Parātpara – Greatest of the Greats
104	ॐ परेशाय नमः om pareś-āya namaḥ	— my obeisance to — Pareśa – Supreme Controller
105	ॐ पारगाय नमः om pāra-gāya namaḥ	— my obeisance to — Pāraga – He who takes His devotees across the Ocean of Births and Deaths
106	ॐ पाराय नमः om pār-āya namaḥ	— my obeisance to — Pāra – Supreme Absolute beyond everything
107	ॐ सर्वदेवात्मकाय नमः om sarva-dev-ātma-kāya namaḥ	— my obeisance to — Sarvadevātmaka – the Soul of all Divinities
108	ॐ परस्मै नमः om paras-mai namaḥ	— my obeisance to — Parasmai – Sovereign God

(Author of this Original Sanskrit Hymn is: Shrī Vyāsa-Deva [Pre-historic Sage]. Translator: Sushma)

श्रीजानकीवल्लभो विजयते

śrījānakīvallabho vijayate

श्रीरामाष्टकम्

śrī-rāmāṣṭakam

सीताराम सीताराम सीताराम सीताराम सीताराम

भजे विशेषसुन्दरं समस्तपापखण्डनम् ।

bhaje viśeṣa-sundaraṁ samasta-pāpa-khaṇḍa-nam ,

स्वभक्तचित्तरञ्जनं सदैव राममद्वयम् ॥ १ ॥

sva-bhakta-citta-rañja-naṁ sa-daiva rāmam-ad-vayam .1.

He, who annihilates all sins, who brings lasting joy to the hearts of His devotees, O mind, dwell upon Him—the supremely beautiful Lord: Shrī Rāma, the One-God second to none.

जटाकलापशोभितं समस्तपापनाशकम् ।

jaṭā-kalā-paśo-bhitaṁ samasta-pāpa-nāśa-kam ,

स्वभक्तभीतिभञ्जनं भजे ह राममद्वयम् ॥ २ ॥

sva-bhakta-bhīti-bhañja-naṁ bhaje ha rāmam-ad-vayam .2.

He, who is the destroyers of sins, who dispels all fears from the hearts of His devotees, O mind, dwell upon His resplendent form with matted hair—Him Shrī Rāma, the One-God second to none.

निजस्वरूपबोधकं कृपाकरं भवापहम् ।

nija-svarūpa-bodha-kaṁ kṛpā-karaṁ bhav-āpaham ,

समं शिवं निरञ्जनं भजे ह राममद्वयम् ॥ ३ ॥

samaṁ śivaṁ nirañja-naṁ bhaje ha rāmam-ad-vayam .3.

Through whom we become enlightened of our true nature, who is most merciful & kind, who takes us across this intimidating ocean-like world, who is equitable to all, who is ever auspicious, ever pure—O mind, dwell upon the ocean of tranquility Shrī Rāma, the One-God second to none.

सहप्रपञ्चकल्पितं ह्यनामरूपवास्तवम् ।

saha-pra-pañca-kalpitaṁ hya-nāma-rūpa-vāsta-vam ,

निराकृतिं निरामयं भजे ह राममद्वयम् ॥ ४ ॥

nir-ākṛtiṁ nir-āmayaṁ bhaje ha rāmam-ad-vayam .4.

Of his will who took this illusory form—who is the world, from whom is the world, who has the world within Him—who is the Absolute-Truth, without a name, without a form, free from blemishes, shortcomings, faults—I worship Him: Shri Rāma, the One-God second to none.

निष्प्रपञ्चनिर्विकल्पनिर्मलं निरामयम् ॥

niṣ-prapañca-nir-vikalpa-nir-malaṁ nirāma-yam.

चिदेकरूपसन्ततं भजे ह राममद्वयम् ॥ ५ ॥

cid-eka-rūpa-santa-taṁ bhaje ha rāmam-ad-vayam .5.

O mind, dwell on Rāma—the imperishable essence beyond creation, beyond the worldly dualities, untainted, the ever pure, unsullied of worldly maladies, the absolute Truth that stands as the all-abiding essence within everything—O mind, worship Rāma, the One-God second to none.

भवाब्धिपोतरूपकं ह्यशेषदेहकल्पितम् ।

bhav-ābdhi-pota-rūpa-kaṁ hya-śeṣa-deha-kal-pitam ,

गुणाकरं कृपाकरं भजे ह राममद्वयम् ॥ ६ ॥

guṇā-karaṁ kṛpā-karaṁ bhaje ha rāmam-ad-vayam .6.

Who is the bark to cross the ocean of worldly existence, the One-shining Truth behind all beingness, doer behind all activity—Him venerate: the all-merciful all-gracious fount of virtues Shrī Rāma, the One-God second to none.

महावाक्यबोधकैर्विराजमनवाक्पदैः ।

mahā-vākya-bodha-kair-virāja-mana-vāk-padaiḥ ,

परब्रह्म व्यापकं भजे ह राममद्वयम् ॥ ७ ॥

para-brahma vyāpa-kaṁ bhaje ha rāmam-ad-vayam .7.

Worship Shrī Rāma—the essence of Vedanta, whose glory irradiates through the great Vedic Sayings, who is the Supreme all-pervading Brahmm diffused throughout the universe—the Exalted One Rāma, the One-God second to none.

शिवप्रदं सुखप्रदं भवच्छिदं भ्रमापहम् ।

śiva-pradaṁ sukha-pradaṁ bhav-acchid-aṁ bhram-āpaham ,

विराजमानदैशिकं भजे ह राममद्वयम् ॥ ८ ॥

virāja-māna-daiśik-aṁ bhaje ha rāmam-ad-vayam .8.

Who confers felicity and prosperity, who rents asunder all worldly bondages, who is beyond the delusive Māyā, who is the Supreme-Self dwelling within His own resplendency—Him I worship, Shrī Rāma, the One-God second to none.

रामाष्टकं पठति यः सुकरं सुपुण्यं

rām-āṣṭakaṁ paṭh-ati yaḥ su-karaṁ su-puṇyaṁ

व्यासेन भाषितमिदं श्रृणुते मनुष्यः ।

vyās-ena bhāṣita-midaṁ śṛṇu-te manuṣ-yaḥ ,

विद्यां श्रियं विपुलसौख्यमनन्तकीर्तिं

vidyāṁ śriyaṁ vipula-saukhyam-ananta-kīrtiṁ

सम्प्राप्य देहविलये लभते च मोक्षम् ॥ ९ ॥

sam-prāpya deha-vilaye labh-ate ca mokṣam .9.

Those who read this octet on Shrī Rāma—easy of comprehension, rife with virtues—which is composed by Sage Vyasa—get abundant knowledge, plentiful wealth, ample happiness, oceanic fame; and they attain to the highest state in the end, gaining emancipation.

॥ इति श्रीव्यासविरचितं रामाष्टकं सम्पूर्णम् ॥

. iti śrī-vyāsa-viraci-taṁ rām-āṣṭakaṁ sam-pūrṇam .

— Thus ends the Ramashtakam composed by Shri Vyasa Maharishi —

(Author of this Original Sanskrit Hymn is: Shrī Vyāsa-Deva [Pre-historic Sage]. Translator: Sushma)

सीताराम
सीताराम सीताराम
सीताराम सीताराम
सीताराम सीताराम

ॐ

सीताराम सीताराम सीताराम
सीताराम सीताराम सीताराम सीताराम सीताराम
सीताराम सीताराम सीताराम सीताराम सीताराम सीताराम

श्रीजानकीवल्लभो विजयते

śrījānakīvallabho vijayate

श्री राम-स्तुति

śrī rāma-stuti

सीताराम सीताराम सीताराम सीताराम सीताराम

श्री रामचन्द्र कृपालु भजु मन हरण भवभय दारुणं,
śrī rāmacandra kṛpālu bhaju mana haraṇa bhavabhaya dāruṇaṁ,
नवकंज-लोचन कंज-मुख कर-कंज पद कंजारुणं.[1]
navakaṁja-locana kaṁja-mukha kara-kaṁja pada kaṁjāruṇaṁ.

O my mind, venerate Lord Rāma, the embodiment of graciousness—who takes one beyond worldly sorrows and pains, beyond fear and beyond neediness—who has eyes like a fresh lotus, and lovely lotus face, as also lotus-like hands and feet.

कंदर्प अगणित अमित छवि नवनील नीरद सुंदरं,
kaṁdarpa agaṇita amita chavi navanīla nīrada suṁdaraṁ,
पट पीत मानहु तड़ित रुचि शुचि नौमि जनक सुतावरं.[2]
paṭa pīta mānahu taṛita ruci śuci naumi janaka sutāvaraṁ.

Having an exquisite form that routs the pride of love-gods infinite, of a beautiful hue that's a new blue—with the likeness of water laden clouds, with his amber-robes which are like flashes of lightning thereon: I venerate that pious Lord of Sīta's soul.

भजु दीनबंधु दिनेश दानव-दैत्य-वंश निकंदनं,
bhaju dīnabaṁdhu dineśa dānava-daitya-vaṁśa nikaṁdanaṁ,
रघुनंद आनँदकंद कोशलचंद दशरथ नंदनं.[3]
raghunaṁda ānam̐dakaṁda kośalacaṁda daśaratha naṁdanaṁ.

O mind, sing the hymns of Shrī Rāma, friend of the poor & destitute, fiery Lord of the Day, who decimated the clans of the wickedly and the night-wandering demons. O chant the name of Raghu-Scion, who's the darling child of Kausalyā, the son of Dasharath: Shrī Rāma, that ocean of blessedness.

सिर मुकुट कुंडल तिलक चारु उदारु अंग विभूषणं,
sira mukuṭa kuṁḍala tilaka cāru udāru aṁga vibhūṣaṇaṁ,
आजानुभुज शर-चाप-धर संग्राम-जित-खरदूषणं.[4]
ājānubhuja śara-cāpa-dhara saṁgrāma-jita-kharadūṣaṇaṁ.

He—whose head bears a crown, with pendants on the ears, a *Tilak* marked on the forehead, whose shapely limbs shine resplendent, whose arms extend down to the knees and wield arms comprising of bow & arrows, who in battle decimated the demons Khara and Dūshan: chant His Holy-Name Rāma, the blissly ocean.

इति वदति तुलसीदास शंकर-शेष-मुनि-मन-रंजनं,
iti vadati tulasīdāsa śaṁkara-śeṣa-muni-mana-raṁjanaṁ,
मम हृदय कंज निवास करु कामादि खल-दल-गंजनं.[5]
mama hṛdaya kaṁja nivāsa karu kāmādi khala-dala-gaṁjanaṁ.

O Shrī Rāma—Joy-of-the-Soul of Shankara, Shesha and other sages; O thou—who decimates the flock-of-vice and their brethren—do please take up thy lotus-like abode in my heart as well: this is the prayer of the servant of your servant—Tulsidās.

श्री रामचन्द्र कृपालु भजु मन हरण भवभय दारुणं ...
śrī rāmacandra kṛpālu bhaju mana haraṇa bhavabhaya dāruṇaṁ ...

(Author of this Original Devanāgri Hymn is: Goswamī Tulsīdās [16th Century Saint]. Translator: Sushma)

सीताराम
सीताराम सीताराम
सीताराम सीताराम
सीताराम सीताराम

ॐ

सीताराम सीताराम सीताराम
सीताराम सीताराम सीताराम सीताराम सीताराम
सीताराम सीताराम सीताराम सीताराम सीताराम सीताराम सीताराम

श्रीजानकीवल्लभो विजयते
śrījānakīvallabho vijayate

श्री हनुमान-स्तुति
śrī hanumāna-stuti

सीताराम सीताराम सीताराम सीताराम सीताराम

मंगल-मूरति मारुत-नंदन, सकल-अमंगल-मूल-निकंदन.[1]
maṁgala-mūrati māruta-naṁdana, sakala-amaṁgala-mūla-nikaṁdana.
पवन-तनय संतन-हितकारी। हृदय विराजत अवध बिहारी.[2]
pavana-tanaya saṁtana-hitakārī, hṛdaya virājata avadha bihārī.
मातु-पिता गुरु गनपति सारद। सिवा-समेत संभु सुक-नारद.[3]
mātu-pitā guru ganapati sārada, sivā-sameta saṁbhu suka-nārada.
चरन बंदि बिनवौं सब काहू। देहु रामपद-नेह-निबाहू.[4]
carana baṁdi binavauṁ saba kāhū, dehu rāmapada-neha-nibāhū.
बंदौं राम-लखन-बैदेही। जे तुलसी के परम सनेही.[5]
baṁdauṁ rāma-lakhana-baidehī, je tulasī ke parama sanehī.
मंगल-मूरति मारुत-नंदन ...
maṁgala-mūrati māruta-naṁdana ...

Venerations to Hanumān, whose sire is Mārut, who is the embodiment of auspiciousness & well-being. Veneration unto him who dispels all faults, and uproots every sin from the very foundation.

Venerations to the Son-of-Wind, who is the great benefactor of saints, in whose heart Lord Shrī Rāma always abides.

I bow my head at the feet of Hanumān, and at the feet of my parents, and my Guru, and goddess Shāradā, and Shri Ganesh; and I bow my head at the feet of Shambhu along with his consort Pārvatī, and at the feet of sages Shukdev and Nārad. I pray to them all and ask them of this boon: Let my devotion for the Holy-Feet of Shrī Rāma always persist steady, firm, undiminished.

And I make many obeisance at the feet of Shrī Rāma, Lakshman, Sītā—who are the most loving benevolent sole Lords of the soul of Tulsidās—who's the servant of their servant.

(Author of this Original Devanāgri Hymn is: Goswamī Tulsīdās [16th Century Saint]. Translator: Sushma)

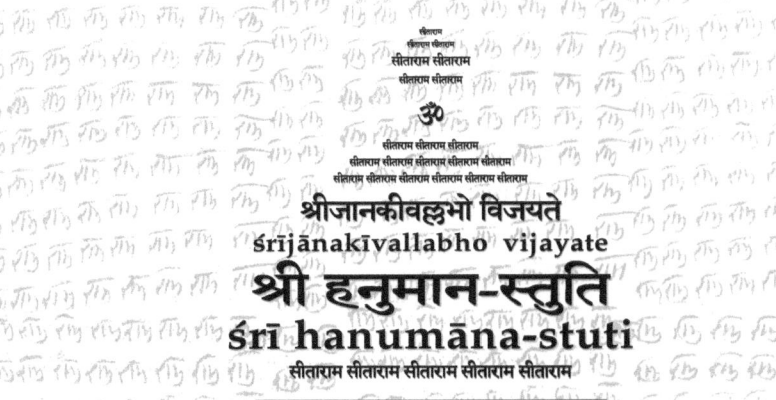

सियावर रामचन्द्र की जय - siyāvara rāmacandra kī jaya
पवनसुत हनुमान की जय - pavanasuta hanumāna kī jaya
गोस्वामी तुलसीदास की जय - gosvāmī tulasīdāsa kī jaya

-- the Following Section Contains Hymns with Devanagari Text & Transliteration Only --

श्रीगणेशपञ्चरत्नस्तोत्रं

-- śrī gaṇeśa-pañcaratna-stotraṁ --

॥ श्रीगणेशाय नमः ॥

-- śrīgaṇeśāya namaḥ --

मुदाकरात्तमोदकं सदाविमुक्तिसाधकं
mudā-karātta-moda-kaṁ sadā-vimukti-sādhakaṁ
कलाधरावतंसकं विलासिलोकरञ्जकम्।
kalā-dharā-vataṁ-sakaṁ vilāsi-loka-rañja-kam ,
अनायकैकनायकं विनाशितेभदैत्यकं
anāya-kaika-nāya-kaṁ vināśite-bhad-aityakaṁ
नताशुभाशुनाशकं नमामि तं विनायकम् ॥ १ ॥
natā-śubhāśu-nāśakaṁ namāmi taṁ vināyakam .1.

नतेतरातिभीकरं नवोदितार्कभास्वरं
nateta-rāti-bhīkaraṁ navodit-ārka-bhā-svaraṁ
नमत्सुरारिनिर्जरं नताधिकापदुद्धरम्।
namat-surāri-nir-jaraṁ nat-ādhik-āpad-uddharam ,
सुरेश्वरं निधीश्वरं गजेश्वरं गणेश्वरं
sureś-varaṁ nidhīś-varaṁ gajeś-varaṁ gaṇeś-varaṁ
महेश्वरं तमाश्रये परात्परं निरन्तरम् ॥ २ ॥
maheś-varaṁ tamāś-raye parāt-paraṁ nir-antaram .2.

समस्तलोकशङ्करं निरस्तदैत्यकुञ्जरं
samasta-loka-śaṅkaraṁ nirasta-daitya-kuñjaraṁ
दरेतरोदरं वरं वरेभवक्त्रमक्षरम्।
dare-taro-daraṁ varaṁ vare-bhav-aktram-akṣaram ,
कृपाकरं क्षमाकरं मुदाकरं यशस्करं
kṛpā-karaṁ kṣamā-karaṁ mudā-karaṁ yaśas-karaṁ
मनस्करं नमस्कृतां नमस्करोमि भास्वरम् ॥ ३ ॥
manas-karaṁ namas-kṛtāṁ namas-karomi bhā-svaram .3.

अकिञ्चनार्तिमार्जनं चिरन्तनोक्तिभाजनं
akiñc-anārtim-ārjanaṁ ciranta-nokti-bhājanaṁ
पुरारिपूर्वनन्दनं सुरारिगर्वचर्वणम्।
purāri-pūrva-nandanaṁ surāri-garva-carva-ṇam ,
प्रपञ्चनाशभीषणं धनञ्जयादिभूषणं
pra-pañca-nāśa-bhīṣa-ṇaṁ dha-nañjay-ādi-bhū-ṣaṇaṁ
कपोलदानवारणं भजे पुराणवारणम् ॥४॥
kapola-dāna-vāraṇaṁ bhaje purāṇa-vāraṇam .4.

नितान्तकान्तदन्तकान्तिमन्तकान्तकात्मजं
nitānta-kānta-danta-kāntim-anta-kānta-kāt-majaṁ
अचिन्त्यरूपमन्तहीनमन्तरायकृन्तनम्।
acintya-rūpa-manta-hīna-manta-rāya-kṛnta-nam ,
हृदन्तरे निरन्तरं वसन्तमेव योगिनां
hṛ-dantare niran-taraṁ vasanta-meva yogi-nāṁ
तमेकदन्तमेव तं विचिन्तयामि सन्ततम् ॥५॥
tameka-danta-meva taṁ vicinta-yāmi santa-tam .5.

महागणेशपञ्चरत्नमादरेण योऽन्वहं
mahā-gaṇeś-pañca-ratna-mā-dareṇa yo-'n-vahaṁ
प्रगायति प्रभातके हृदि स्मरन् गणेश्वरम्।
pragā-yati prabhā-take hṛdi smaran gaṇeś-varam ,
अरोगतामदोषतां सुसाहितीं सुपुत्रतां
aroga-tāma-doṣa-tāṁ susā-hitīṁ su-putra-tāṁ
समाहितायुरष्टभूतिमभ्युपैति सोऽचिरात् ॥६॥
samā-hitā-yuraṣṭa-bhūtim-abhyu-paiti so-'ci-rāt .6.

॥ इति श्रीशङ्करभगवतः कृतौ श्रीगणेशपञ्चरत्नस्तोत्रं सम्पूर्णम् ॥
. iti śrī-śaṅkara-bhagavataḥ kṛtau śrī-gaṇeśa-pañca-ratna-stotraṁ sampūrṇam .

शिव नाम जप

— śiva nāma japa —

नमः शिवाय । नमः शिवाय । ॐ नमः शिवाय ।

namaḥ śivāya - namaḥ śivāya - om namaḥ śivāya

ॐ नमः शिवाय ॐ नमः शिवाय । हर हर भोले नमः शिवाय ॥

om namaḥ śivāya om namaḥ śivāya - hara hara bhole namaḥ śivāya

महाकालेश्वराय महाकालेश्वराय । हर हर भोले नमः शिवाय ॥

mahā-kāleśvarāya mahākāleśvarāya - hara hara bhole namaḥ śivāya

ॐ सोमेश्वराय शिव सोमेश्वराय । हर हर भोले नमः शिवाय ॥

om someśvarāya śiva someśvarāya - hara hara bhole namaḥ śivāya

जटाधराय शिव जटाधराय । हर हर भोले नमः शिवाय ॥

jaṭādharāya śiva jaṭādharāya - hara hara bhole namaḥ śivāya

ॐ रामेशवराय शिव रामेशवराय । हर हर भोले नमः शिवाय ॥

om rāmeśavarāya śiva rāmeśavarāya - hara hara bhole namaḥ śivāya

गंगाधराय शिव गंगाधराय । हर हर भोले नमः शिवाय ॥

gaṁgādharāya śiva gaṁgādharāya , hara hara bhole namaḥ śivāya

ॐ विश्वेशवराय शिव विश्वेशवराय । हर हर भोले नमः शिवाय ॥

om viśveśavarāya śiva viśveśavarāya - hara hara bhole namaḥ śivāya

कोटेश्वराय शिव कोटेश्वराय । हर हर भोले नमः शिवाय ॥

koṭeśvarāya śiva koṭeśvarāya - hara hara bhole namaḥ śivāya

श्री रामायण आरती — śrī rāmāyaṇa āratī

आरति श्रीरामायनजी की, कीरति कलित ललित सिय पी की.
ārati śrīrāmāyanajī kī, kīrati kalita lalita siya pī kī.

गावत ब्रह्मादिक मुनि नारद, बालमीक बिग्यान बिसारद.
gāvata brahmādika muni nārada, bālamīka bigyāna bisārada.
सुक सनकादि सेष अरु सारद, बरनि पवनसुत कीरति नीकी.१.
suka sanakādi seṣa aru sārada, barani pavanasuta kīrati nīkī. [1]

गावत बेद पुरान अष्टदस, छओ सास्त्र सब ग्रंथन को रस.
gāvata beda purāna aṣṭadasa, chao sāstra saba graṁthana ko rasa.
मुनि जन धन संतन को सरबस, सार अंस संमत सबही की.२.
muni jana dhana saṁtana ko sarabasa, sāra aṁsa saṁmata sabahī kī. [2]

गावत संतत संभु भवानी, अरु घटसंभव मुनि बिग्यानी.
gāvata saṁtata saṁbhu bhavānī, aru ghaṭasaṁbhava muni bigyānī.
ब्यास आदि कबिबर्ज बखानी, कागभुसुंडि गरुड के ही की.३.
byāsa ādi kabibarja bakhānī, kāgabhusuṁḍi garuḍa ke hī kī. [3]

कलिमल हरनि बिषय रस फीकी, सुभग सिंगार मुक्ति जुबती की.
kalimala harani biṣaya rasa phīkī, subhaga siṁgāra mukti jubatī kī.
दलन रोग भव मूरि अमी की, तात मात सब बिधि तुलसी की.४.
dalana roga bhava mūri amī kī, tāta māta saba bidhi tulasī kī. [4]

आरति श्रीरामायनजी की, कीरति कलित ललित सिय पी की ...
ārati śrīrāmāyanajī kī, kīrati kalita lalita siya pī kī ...

जय जगदीश हरे आरती -- jaya jagadīśa hare āratī

ॐ जय जगदीश हरे
om jaya jagadīśa hare
स्वामी जय जगदीश हरे
swāmī jaya jagadīśa hare
भक्त जनों के संकट
bhakta janoṅ ke saṅkaṭa
दास जनों के संकट
dāsa janoṅ ke saṅkaṭa
क्षण में दूर करे
kṣaṇa meṅ dūra kare
ॐ जय जगदीश हरे
om jaya jagadīśa hare
जो ध्यावे फल पावे
jo dhyāve phala pāve
दुख बिनसे मन का
dukha binase mana kā
स्वामी दुख बिनसे मन का
swāmī dukha binase mana kā
सुख सम्पति घर आवे
sukha sampatī ghara āve
सुख सम्पति घर आवे
sukha sampatī ghara āve
कष्ट मिटे तन का
kaṣṭa miṭe tana kā
ॐ जय जगदीश हरे
om jaya jagadīśa hare
मात पिता तुम मेरे
māta pitā tuma mere
शरण गहूं किसकी
śaraṇa gahūṅ kisakī

स्वामी शरण गहूं मैं किसकी
swāmi śaraṇa gahūṅ maiṅ kisakī
तुम बिन और न दूजा
tuma bina aura na dūjā
हरि बिन और न दूजा
hari bina aura na dūjā
आस करूं मैं जिसकी
āsa karūṇ maiṅ jisakī
ॐ जय जगदीश हरे
om jaya jagadīśa hare
तुम पूरण परमात्मा
tuma pūraṇa paramātmā
तुम अंतरयामी
tuma aṅtarayāmī
स्वामी तुम अंतरयामी
swāmi tuma aṅtarayāmī
पारब्रह्म परमेश्वर
pārabrahma parameśwara
पारब्रह्म परमेश्वर
pārabrahma parameśwara
तुम सब के स्वामी
tuma saba ke swāmī
ॐ जय जगदीश हरे
om jaya jagadīśa hare
तुम करुणा के सागर
tuma karuṇā ke sāgara
तुम पालनकर्ता
tuma pālanakartā
स्वामी तुम पालनकर्ता
swāmī tuma pālanakartā

मैं मूरख खल कामी
maiṅ mūrakh khala kāmī
मैं सेवक तुम स्वामी
maiṅ sevaka tuma swāmī
कृपा करो भर्ता
kṛpā karo bhartā
ॐ जय जगदीश हरे
om jaya jagadīśa hare

तुम हो एक अगोचर
tuma ho eka agochara
सबके प्राणपति
sabake prāṇapati
स्वामी सबके प्राणपति
swāmī sabake prāṇapati
किस विधि मिलूं दयामय
kisa vidhi milūṅ dayāmaya
किस विधि मिलूं दयामय
kisa vidhi milūṅ dayāmaya
तुमको मैं कुमति
tumako maiṅ kumati
ॐ जय जगदीश हरे
om jaya jagadīśa hare

दीनबंधु दुखहर्ता
dīnabaṅdhu dukhahartā
ठाकुर तुम मेरे
ṭhākura tuma mere
स्वामी रक्षक तुम मेरे
swāmī rakṣaka tuma mere
अपने हस्त उठाओ
apane hasta uṭhāo
अपनी शरण लगाओ
apanī śaraṇa lagāo
द्वार पड़ा मै तेरे
dwāra paṛā mai tere
ॐ जय जगदीश हरे
om jaya jagadīśa hare

विषय विकार मिटाओ
viṣaya vikāra miṭāo
पाप हरो देवा
pāpa haro devā
स्वमी कष्ट हरो देवा
swāmī kaṣṭa haro devā
श्रद्धा भक्ति बढ़ाओ
śraddhā bhakti baṛhāo
श्रद्धा प्रेम बढ़ाओ
śraddhā prema baṛhāo
संतन की सेवा
saṅtana kī sevā
ॐ जय जगदीश हरे
om jaya jagadīśa hare

ॐ जय जगदीश हरे
om jaya jagdīśa hare
स्वामी जय जगदीश हरे
swāmī jaya jagadīśa hare
भक्त जनों के संकट
bhakta janoṅ ke saṅkaṭa
दास जनों के संकट
dāsa janoṅ ke saṅkaṭa
क्षण में दूर करे
kṣaṇa meṅ dūra kare
ॐ जय जगदीश हरे
om jaya jagadīśa hare

श्री हनुमान चालीसा — śrī hanumāna cālīsā [single-page]

दोहा - dohā

श्रीगुरु चरन सरोज रज निज मन मुकुर सुधारि, बरनऊँ रघुबर बिमल जस जो दायक फल चारि.
śrīguru carana saroja raja nija mana mukura sudhāri, baranaūṁ raghubara bimala jasa jo dāyaka phala cāri.
बुद्धि हीन तनु जानिकै सुमिरौं पवन कुमार, बल बुद्धि बिद्या देहु मोहि हरहु कलेश विकार.
buddhi hīna tanu jānikai sumirauṁ pavana kumāra, bala buddhi bidyā dehu mohi harahu kaleśa vikāra.

चौपाई - caupāī

जय हनुमान ज्ञान गुण सागर, जय कपीश तिहुँ लोक उजागर. 1
jaya hanumāna jñāna guṇa sāgara, jaya kapīśa tihuṁ loka ujāgara.
राम दूत अतुलित बल धामा, अंजनिपुत्र पवनसुत नामा. 2
rāma dūta atulita bala dhāmā, aṁjaniputra pavanasuta nāmā.
महाबीर बिक्रम बजरंगी, कुमति निवार सुमति के संगी. 3
mahābīra bikrama bajaraṁgī, kumati nivāra sumati ke saṁgī.
कंचन बरन बिराज सुबेषा, कानन कुंडल कुंचित केशा. 4
kaṁcana barana birāja subeṣā, kānana kuṁḍala kuṁcita keśā.
हाथ बज्र और ध्वजा बिराजै, काँधे मूँज जनेऊ साजै. 5
hātha bajra aura dhvajā birājai, kāṁdhe mūṁja janeū sājai.
शङ्कर स्वयं केशरीनंदन, तेज प्रताप महा जग बंदन. 6
śaṅkara svayaṁ keśarīnaṁdana, teja pratāpa mahā jaga baṁdana.
विद्यावान गुणी अति चातुर, राम काज करिबे को आतुर. 7
vidyāvāna guṇī ati cātura, rāma kāja karibe ko ātura.
प्रभु चरित्र सुनिबे को रसिया, राम लखन सीता मन बसिया. 8
prabhu caritra sunibe ko rasiyā, rāma lakhana sītā mana basiyā.
सूक्ष्म रूप धरि सियहिं दिखावा, बिकट रूप धरि लंक जरावा. 9
sūkṣma rūpa dhari siyahiṁ dikhāvā, bikaṭa rūpa dhari laṁka jarāvā.
भीम रूप धरि असुर सँहारे, रामचन्द्र के काज सँवारे. 10
bhīma rūpa dhari asura saṁhāre, rāmacandra ke kāja saṁvāre.
लाय संजीवनि लखन जियाये, श्री रघुबीर हरषि उर लाये. 11
lāya saṁjīvani lakhana jiyāye, śrī raghubīra haraṣi ura lāye.
रघुपति कीन्ही बहुत बड़ाई, तुम मम प्रिय भरतहिं सम भाई. 12
raghupati kīnhī bahuta baṛāī, tuma mama priya bharatahiṁ sama bhāī.
सहस बदन तुम्हरो जस गावैं, अस कहि श्रीपति कंठ लगावैं. 13
sahasa badana tumharo jasa gāvaiṁ, asa kahi śrīpati kaṁṭha lagāvaiṁ.
सनकादिक ब्रह्मादि मुनीशा, नारद शारद सहित अहीशा. 14
sanakādika brahmādi munīśā, nārada śārada sahita ahīśā.
जम कुबेर दिगपाल जहाँ ते, कबि कोबिद कहि सकै कहाँ ते. 15
jama kubera digapāla jahāṁ te, kabi kobida kahi sakai kahāṁ te.
तुम उपकार सुग्रीवहिं कीन्हा, राम मिलाय राज पद दीन्हा. 16
tuma upakāra sugrīvahiṁ kīnhā, rāma milāya rāja pada dīnhā.
तुम्हरो मंत्र बिभीषन माना, लंकेश्वर भए सब जग जाना. 17
tumharo maṁtra bibhīṣana mānā, laṁkeśvara bhae saba jaga jānā.
जुग सहस्त्र जोजन पर भानू, लील्यो ताहि मधुर फल जानू. 18
* juga sahastra jojana para bhānū, līlyo tāhi madhura phala jānū.
प्रभु मुद्रिका मेलि मुख माहीं, जलधि लाँघि गये अचरज नाहीं. 19
prabhu mudrikā meli mukha māhīṁ, jaladhi lāṁghi gaye acaraja nāhīṁ.
दुर्गम काज जगत के जेते, सुगम अनुग्रह तुम्हरे तेते. 20
durgama kāja jagata ke jete, sugama anugraha tumhare tete.

राम दुआरे तुम रखवारे, होत न आज्ञा बिनु पैसारे. 21
rāma duāre tuma rakhavāre, hota na ājñā binu paisāre.
सब सुख लहैं तुम्हारी शरना, तुम रक्षक काहू को डर ना. 22
saba sukha lahaiṁ tumhārī śaranā, tuma rakṣaka kāhū ko ḍara nā.
आपन तेज सम्हारो आपै, तीनौं लोक हाँक ते काँपै. 23
āpana teja samhāro āpai, tīnauṁ loka hāṁka te kāṁpai.
भूत पिशाच निकट नहिं आवै, महाबीर जब नाम सुनावै. 24
bhūta piśāca nikaṭa nahiṁ āvai, mahābīra jaba nāma sunāvai.
नासै रोग हरै सब पीरा, जपत निरंतर हनुमत बीरा. 25
nāsai roga harai saba pīrā, japata niraṁtara hanumata bīrā.
संकट ते हनुमान छुड़ावै, मन क्रम बचन ध्यान जो लावै. 26
saṁkaṭa te hanumāna chuṛāvai, mana krama bacana dhyāna jo lāvai.
सब पर राम तपस्वी राजा, तिन के काज सकल तुम साजा. 27
saba para rāma tapasvī rājā, tina ke kāja sakala tuma sājā.
और मनोरथ जो कोउ लावै, तासु अमित जीवन फल पावै. 28
aura manoratha jo kou lāvai, tāsu amita jīvana phala pāvai.
चारों जुग परताप तुम्हारा, है परसिद्ध जगत उजियारा. 29
cāroṁ juga paratāpa tumhārā, hai parasiddha jagata ujiyārā.
साधु संत के तुम रखवारे, असुर निकंदन राम दुलारे. 30
sādhu saṁta ke tuma rakhavāre, asura nikaṁdana rāma dulāre.
अष्ट सिद्धि नव निधि के दाता, अस बर दीन्ह जानकी माता. 31
aṣṭa siddhi nava nidhi ke dātā, asa bara dīnha jānakī mātā.
राम रसायन तुम्हरे पासा, सदा रहउ रघुपति के दासा. 32
rāma rasāyana tumhare pāsā, sadā rahau raghupati ke dāsā.
तुम्हरे भजन राम को पावै, जनम जनम के दुख बिसरावै. 33
tumhare bhajana rāma ko pāvai, janama janama ke dukha bisarāvai.
अंत काल रघुबर पुर जाई, जहाँ जन्म हरिभक्त कहाई. 34
aṁta kāla raghubara pura jāī, jahāṁ janma haribhakta kahāī.
और देवता चित्त न धरई, हनुमत सेइ सर्ब सुख करई. 35
aura devatā citta na dharaī, hanumata sei sarba sukha karaī.
संकट कटै मिटै सब पीरा, जो सुमिरै हनुमत बलबीरा. 36
saṁkaṭa kaṭai miṭai saba pīrā, jo sumirai hanumata balabīrā.
जय जय जय हनुमान गोसाईं, कृपा करहु गुरु देव की नाईं. 37
jaya jaya jaya hanumāna gosāīṁ, kṛpā karahu guru deva kī nāīṁ.
यह शत बार पाठ कर जोई, छूटै बंदि महा सुख सोई. 38
yaha śata bāra pāṭha kara joī, chūṭai baṁdi mahā sukha soī.
जो यह पढ़ै हनुमान चालीसा, होय सिद्धि साखी गौरीसा. 39
jo yaha paṛhai hanumāna cālīsā, hoya siddhi sākhī gaurīsā.
तुलसीदास सदा हरि चेरा, कीजै नाथ हृदय महँ डेरा. 40
tulasīdāsa sadā hari cerā, kījai nātha hṛdaya mahaṁ ḍerā.

दोहा - dohā

पवन तनय संकट हरन मंगल मूरति रूप, राम लखन सीता सहित हृदय बसहु सुर भूप.
pavana tanaya saṁkaṭa harana maṁgala mūrati rūpa, rāma lakhana sītā sahita hṛdaya basahu sura bhūpa.

* Here Juga (which equal 12,000 Divine-Years per Vedic-Time-Scale) is used as a number; sahastra is 1000; jojana is 8 miles. The distance to Bhanu (Sun) 12,000x1000x8 = 96 million miles is given out in this 18th Chaupai. This estimate by Tulsīdās from sixteenth century India is within 3.3% of modern day calculations.

(Devanagari Text Only)

For the benefits of
Expert Hindi Readers
—who may wish to read the Hymns
uninterrupted of
Transliteration & Translation—
we have,
in the Next Section,
repeated the Original Texts
in
Devanagari Script Only
—for a speedy recital

दोहा - dohā

श्रीगुरु चरन सरोज रज निज मन मुकुर सुधारि ।
बरनऊँ रघुबर बिमल जस जो दायक फल चारि ॥
बुद्धि हीन तनु जानिकै सुमिरौं पवन कुमार ।
बल बुद्धि बिद्या देहु मोहि हरहु कलेश विकार ॥

चौपाई - caupāī

जय हनुमान ज्ञान गुण सागर । जय कपीश तिहुँ लोक उजागर ॥ 1
राम दूत अतुलित बल धामा । अंजनिपुत्र पवनसुत नामा ॥ 2
महाबीर बिक्रम बजरंगी । कुमति निवार सुमति के संगी ॥ 3
कंचन बरन बिराज सुबेषा । कानन कुंडल कुंचित केशा ॥ 4
हाथ बज्र और ध्वजा बिराजै । काँधे मूँज जनेऊ साजै ॥ 5
शङ्कर स्वयं केशरीनंदन । तेज प्रताप महा जग बंदन ॥ 6
विद्यावान गुणी अति चातुर । राम काज करिबे को आतुर ॥ 7
प्रभु चरित्र सुनिबे को रसिया । राम लखन सीता मन बसिया ॥ 8
सूक्ष्म रूप धरि सियहिं दिखावा । बिकट रूप धरि लंक जरावा ॥ 9
भीम रूप धरि असुर सँहारे । रामचन्द्र के काज सँवारे ॥ 10
लाय संजीवनि लखन जियाये । श्री रघुबीर हरषि उर लाये ॥ 11
रघुपति कीन्ही बहुत बड़ाई । तुम मम प्रिय भरतहिं सम भाई ॥ 12
सहस बदन तुम्हरो जस गावैं । अस कहि श्रीपति कंठ लगावैं ॥ 13
सनकादिक ब्रह्मादि मुनीशा । नारद शारद सहित अहीशा ॥ 14
जम कुबेर दिगपाल जहाँ ते । कबि कोबिद कहि सकै कहाँ ते ॥ 15
तुम उपकार सुग्रीवहिं कीन्हा । राम मिलाय राज पद दीन्हा ॥ 16
तुम्हरो मंत्र बिभीषन माना । लंकेश्वर भए सब जग जाना ॥ 17
जुग सहस्त्र जोजन पर भानू । लील्यो ताहि मधुर फल जानू ॥ 18
प्रभु मुद्रिका मेलि मुख माहीं । जलधि लाँघि गये अचरज नाहीं ॥ 19

दुर्गम काज जगत के जेते । सुगम अनुग्रह तुम्हरे तेते ॥ 20

राम दुआरे तुम रखवारे । होत न आज्ञा बिनु पैसारे ॥ 21

सब सुख लहैं तुम्हारी शरना । तुम रक्षक काहू को डर ना ॥ 22

आपन तेज सम्हारो आपै । तीनौं लोक हाँक ते काँपै ॥ 23

भूत पिशाच निकट नहिं आवै । महाबीर जब नाम सुनावै ॥ 24

नासै रोग हरै सब पीरा । जपत निरंतर हनुमत बीरा ॥ 25

संकट ते हनुमान छुडावै । मन क्रम बचन ध्यान जो लावै ॥ 26

सब पर राम तपस्वी राजा । तिन के काज सकल तुम साजा ॥ 27

और मनोरथ जो कोउ लावै । तासु अमित जीवन फल पावै ॥ 28

चारों जुग परताप तुम्हारा । है परसिद्ध जगत उजियारा ॥ 29

साधु संत के तुम रखवारे । असुर निकंदन राम दुलारे ॥ 30

अष्ट सिद्धि नव निधि के दाता । अस बर दीन्ह जानकी माता ॥ 31

राम रसायन तुम्हरे पासा । सदा रहउ रघुपति के दासा ॥ 32

तुम्हरे भजन राम को पावै । जनम जनम के दुख बिसरावै ॥ 33

अंत काल रघुबर पुर जाई । जहाँ जन्म हरिभक्त कहाई ॥ 34

और देवता चित्त न धरई । हनुमत सेइ सर्ब सुख करई ॥ 35

संकट कटै मिटै सब पीरा । जो सुमिरै हनुमत बलबीरा ॥ 36

जय जय जय हनुमान गोसाईं । कृपा करहु गुरु देव की नाईं ॥ 37

यह शत बार पाठ कर जोई । छूटै बंदि महा सुख सोई ॥ 38

जो यह पढ़ै हनुमान चालीसा । होय सिद्धि साखी गौरीसा ॥ 39

तुलसीदास सदा हरि चेरा । कीजै नाथ हृदय महँ डेरा ॥ 40

दोहा - dohā

पवन तनय संकट हरन मंगल मूरति रूप ।

राम लखन सीता सहित हृदय बसहु सुर भूप ॥

ॐ

अस्य श्रीरामरक्षास्तोत्रमन्त्रस्य बुधकौशिक ऋषिः
श्रीसीतारामचन्द्रो देवता अनुष्टुप् छन्दः
सीता शक्तिः श्रीमान् हनुमान् कीलकं
श्रीरामचन्द्रप्रीत्यर्थे रामरक्षास्तोत्रजपे विनियोगः ॥

-- अथ ध्यानम् --

ध्यायेदाजानुबाहुं धृतशरधनुषं बद्धपद्मासनस्थं
पीतं वासो वसानं नवकमलदलस्पर्धिनेत्रं प्रसन्नम् ।
वामाङ्कारूढसीतामुखकमलमिलल्लोचनं नीरदाभं
नानालंकारदीप्तं दधतमुरुजटामण्डलं रामचन्द्रम् ॥

-- इति ध्यानम् --

चरितं रघुनाथस्य शतकोटि प्रविस्तरम् ।
एकैकमक्षरं पुंसां महापातकनाशनम् ॥ १ ॥
ध्यात्वा नीलोत्पलश्यामं रामं राजीवलोचनम् ।
जानकीलक्ष्मणोपेतं जटामुकुटमण्डितम् ॥ २ ॥
सासितूणधनुर्बाणपाणिं नक्तंचरान्तकम् ।
स्वलीलया जगत्त्रातुमविर्भूतमजं विभुम् ॥ ३ ॥
रामरक्षां पठेत्प्राज्ञः पापघ्नीं सर्वकामदाम् ।
शिरो मे राघवः पातु भालं दशरथात्मजः ॥ ४ ॥
कौसल्येयो दृशौ पातु विश्वामित्रप्रियः श्रुती ।
घ्राणं पातु मखत्राता मुखं सौमित्रिवत्सलः ॥ ५ ॥
जिह्वां विद्यानिधिः पातु कण्ठं भरतवंदितः ।
स्कन्धौ दिव्यायुधः पातु भुजौ भग्नेशकार्मुकः ॥ ६ ॥

करौ सीतापतिः पातु हृदयं जामदग्न्यजित् ।
मध्यं पातु खरध्वंसी नाभिं जाम्बवदाश्रयः ॥ ७ ॥
सुग्रीवेशः कटी पातु सक्थिनी हनुमत्प्रभुः ।
ऊरू रघूत्तमः पातु रक्षःकुलविनाशकृत् ॥ ८ ॥
जानुनी सेतुकृत्पातु जङ्घे दशमुखान्तकः ।
पादौ बिभीषणश्रीदः पातु रामोऽखिलं वपुः ॥ ९ ॥
एतां रामबलोपेतां रक्षां यः सुकृती पठेत् ।
स चिरायुः सुखी पुत्री विजयी विनयी भवेत् ॥ १० ॥
पातालभूतलव्योमचारिणश्छद्मचारिणः ।
न द्रष्टुमपि शक्तास्ते रक्षितं रामनामभिः ॥ ११ ॥
रामेति रामभद्रेति रामचन्द्रेति वा स्मरन् ।
नरो न लिप्यते पापैर्भुक्तिं मुक्तिं च विन्दति ॥ १२ ॥
जगज्जैत्रेकमन्त्रेण रामनाम्नाऽभिरक्षितम् ।
यः कण्ठे धारयेत्तस्य करस्थाः सर्वसिद्धयः ॥ १३ ॥
वज्रपंजरनामेदं यो रामकवचं स्मरेत् ।
अव्याहताज्ञः सर्वत्र लभते जयमंगलम् ॥ १४ ॥
आदिष्टवान्यथा स्वप्ने रामरक्षामिमां हरः ।
तथा लिखितवान्प्रातः प्रभुद्धो बुधकौशिकः ॥ १५ ॥
आरामः कल्पवृक्षाणां विरामः सकलापदाम् ।
अभिरामस्त्रिलोकानां रामः श्रीमान्स नः प्रभुः ॥ १६ ॥
तरुणौ रूपसम्पन्नौ सुकुमारौ महाबलौ ।
पुण्डरीकविशालाक्षौ चीरकृष्णाजिनाम्बरौ ॥ १७ ॥
फलमूलाशिनौ दान्तौ तापसौ ब्रह्मचारिणौ ।
पुत्रौ दशरथस्यैतौ भ्रातरौ रामलक्ष्मणौ ॥ १८ ॥

शरण्यौ सर्वसत्त्वानां श्रेष्ठौ सर्वधनुष्मताम् ।
रक्षः कुलनिहन्तारौ त्रायेतां नो रघूत्तमौ ॥ १९ ॥
आत्तसज्जधनुषाविषुस्पृशावक्षयाशुगनिषङ्गसङ्गनौ ।
रक्षणाय मम रामलक्ष्मणावग्रतः पथि सदैव गच्छताम् ॥ २० ॥
संनद्धः कवची खड्गी चापबाणधरो युवा ।
गच्छन्मनोरथान्नश्च रामः पातु सलक्ष्मणः ॥ २१ ॥
रामो दाशरथिः शूरो लक्ष्मणानुचरो बली ।
काकुत्स्थः पुरुषः पूर्णः कौसल्येयो रघूत्तमः ॥ २२ ॥
वेदान्तवेद्यो यज्ञेशः पुराणपुरुषोत्तमः ।
जानकीवल्लभः श्रीमान् अप्रमेय पराक्रमः ॥ २३ ॥
इत्येतानि जपन्नित्यं मद्भक्तः श्रद्धयान्वितः ।
अश्वमेधाधिकं पुण्यं सम्प्राप्नोति न संशयः ॥ २४ ॥
रामं दुर्वादलश्यामं पद्माक्षं पीतवाससम् ।
स्तुवन्ति नामभिर्दिव्यैर्न ते संसारिणो नराः ॥ २५ ॥
रामं लक्ष्मणपूर्वजं रघुवरं सीतापतिं सुन्दरं
काकुत्स्थं करुणार्णवं गुणनिधिं विप्रप्रियं धार्मिकम् ।
राजेन्द्रं सत्यसंधं दशरथतनयं श्यामलं शान्तमूर्तिं
वन्दे लोकाभिरामं रघुकुलतिलकं राघवं रावणारिम् ॥ २६ ॥
रामाय रामभद्राय रामचन्द्राय वेधसे ।
रघुनाथाय नाथाय सीतायाः पतये नमः ॥ २७ ॥
श्रीराम राम रघुनन्दन राम राम - श्रीराम राम भरताग्रज राम राम ।
श्रीराम राम रणकर्कश राम राम - श्रीराम राम शरणं भव राम राम ॥ २८ ॥
श्रीरामचन्द्रचरणौ मनसा स्मरामि - श्रीरामचन्द्रचरणौ वचसा गृणामि ।
श्रीरामचन्द्रचरणौ शिरसा नमामि - श्रीरामचन्द्रचरणौ शरणं प्रपद्ये ॥ २९ ॥

माता रामो मत्पिता रामचन्द्रः - स्वामी रामो मत्सखा रामचन्द्रः ।
सर्वस्वं मे रामचन्द्रो दयालु - र्नान्यं जाने नैव जाने न जाने ॥ ३० ॥

दक्षिणे लक्ष्मणो यस्य वामे च जनकात्मजा ।
पुरतो मारुतिर्यस्य तं वन्दे रघुनन्दनम् ॥ ३१ ॥

लोकाभिरामं रणरङ्गधीरं - राजीवनेत्रं रघुवंशनाथम् ।
कारुण्यरूपं करुणाकरं तं - श्रीरामचन्द्रं शरणं प्रपद्ये ॥ ३२ ॥

मनोजवं मारुततुल्यवेगं - जितेन्द्रियं बुद्धिमतां वरिष्ठम् ।
वातात्मजं वानरयूथमुख्यं - श्रीरामदूतं शरणं प्रपद्ये ॥ ३३ ॥

कूजन्तं रामरामेति मधुरं मधुराक्षरम् ।
आरुह्य कविताशाखां वन्दे वाल्मीकिकोकिलम् ॥ ३४ ॥

आपदामपहर्तारं दातारं सर्वसम्पदाम् ।
लोकाभिरामं श्रीरामं भूयो भूयो नमाम्यहम् ॥ ३५ ॥

भर्जनं भवबीजानामर्जनं सुखसम्पदाम् ।
तर्जनं यमदूतानां रामरामेति गर्जनम् ॥ ३६ ॥

रामो राजमणिः सदा विजयते रामं रमेशं भजे
रामेणाभिहता निशाचरचमू रामाय तस्मै नमः ।
रामान्नास्ति परायणं परतरं रामस्य दासोऽस्म्यहं
रामे चित्तलयः सदा भवतु मे भो राम मामुद्धर ॥ ३७ ॥

राम रामेति रामेति रमे रामे मनोरमे ।
सहस्रनाम तत्तुल्यं रामनाम वरानने ॥ ३८ ॥

॥ इति श्रीबुधकौशिकमुनिविरचितं श्रीरामरक्षास्तोत्रं सम्पूर्णम् ॥

दोहा-dohā:

नाथ कृतारथ भयउँ मैं तव दरसन खगराज ।
आयसु देहु सो करौं अब प्रभु आयहु केहि काज ॥६३क॥
सदा कृतारथ रूप तुम्ह कह मृदु बचन खगेस ।
जेहि कै अस्तुति सादर निज मुख कीन्हि महेस ॥६३ख॥

चौपाई-caupāī:

सुनहु तात जेहि कारन आयउँ । सो सब भयउ दरस तव पायउँ ॥
देखि परम पावन तव आश्रम । गयउ मोह संसय नाना भ्रम ॥
अब श्रीराम कथा अति पावनि । सदा सुखद दुख पुंज नसावनि ॥
सादर तात सुनावहु मोही । बार बार बिनवउँ प्रभु तोही ॥
सुनत गरुड़ कै गिरा बिनीता । सरल सुप्रेम सुखद सुपुनीता ॥
भयउ तासु मन परम उछाहा । लाग कहै रघुपति गुन गाहा ॥
प्रथमहिं अति अनुराग भवानी । रामचरित सर कहेसि बखानी ॥
पुनि नारद कर मोह अपारा । कहेसि बहुरि रावन अवतारा ॥
प्रभु अवतार कथा पुनि गाई । तब सिसु चरित कहेसि मन लाई ॥

दोहा-dohā:

बालचरित कहि बिबिधि बिधि मन महँ परम उछाह ।
रिषि आगवन कहेसि पुनि श्रीरघुबीर बिबाह ॥६४॥

चौपाई-caupāī:

बहुरि राम अभिषेक प्रसंगा । पुनि नृप बचन राज रस भंगा ॥
पुरबासिन्ह कर बिरह बिषादा । कहेसि राम लछिमन संबादा ॥
बिपिन गवन केवट अनुरागा । सुरसरि उतरि निवास प्रयागा ॥
बालमीक प्रभु मिलन बखाना । चित्रकूट जिमि बसे भगवाना ॥
सचिवागवन नगर नृप मरना । भरतागवन प्रेम बहु बरना ॥
करि नृप क्रिया संग पुरबासी । भरत गए जहँ प्रभु सुख रासी ॥
पुनि रघुपति बहुबिधि समुझाए । लै पादुका अवधपुर आए ॥
भरत रहनि सुरपति सुत करनी । प्रभु अरु अत्रि भेंट पुनि बरनी ॥

दोहा-dohā:

कहि बिराध बध जेहि बिधि देह तजी सरभंग ।
बरनि सुतीछन प्रीति पुनि प्रभु अगस्ति सतसंग ॥६५॥

चौपाई-caupāī:

कहि दंडक बन पावनताई । गीध मइत्री पुनि तेहिं गाई ॥
पुनि प्रभु पंचबटीं कृत बासा । भंजी सकल मुनिन्ह की त्रासा ॥
पुनि लछिमन उपदेस अनूपा । सूपनखा जिमि कीन्हि कुरूपा ॥
खर दूषन बध बहुरि बखाना । जिमि सब मरमु दसानन जाना ॥
दसकंधर मारीच बतकही । जेहि बिधि भई सो सब तेहिं कही ॥

पुनि माया सीता कर हरना । श्रीरघुबीर बिरह कछु बरना ॥
पुनि प्रभु गीध क्रिया जिमि कीन्ही । बधि कबंध सबरिहि गति दीन्ही ॥
बहुरि बिरह बरनत रघुबीरा । जेहि बिधि गए सरोबर तीरा ॥

दोहा-dohā:

प्रभु नारद संबाद कहि मारुति मिलन प्रसंग ।
पुनि सुग्रीव मिताई बालि प्रान कर भंग ॥६६क॥
कपिहि तिलक करि प्रभु कृत सैल प्रबरषन बास ।
बरनन बर्षा सरद अरु राम रोष कपि त्रास ॥६६ख॥

चौपाई-caupāī:

जेहि बिधि कपिपति कीस पठाए । सीता खोज सकल दिसि धाए ॥
बिबर प्रबेस कीन्ह जेहि भाँती । कपिन्ह बहोरि मिला संपाती ॥
सुनि सब कथा समीरकुमारा । नाघत भयउ पयोधि अपारा ॥
लंकाँ कपि प्रबेस जिमि कीन्हा । पुनि सीतहि धीरजु जिमि दीन्हा ॥
बन उजारि रावनहि प्रबोधी । पुर दहि नाघेउ बहुरि पयोधी ॥
आए कपि सब जहँ रघुराई । बैदेही कि कुसल सुनाई ॥
सेन समेति जथा रघुबीरा । उतरे जाइ बारिनिधि तीरा ॥
मिला बिभीषन जेहि बिधि आई । सागर निग्रह कथा सुनाई ॥

दोहा-dohā:

सेतु बाँधि कपि सेन जिमि उतरी सागर पार ।
गयउ बसीठी बीरबर जेहि बिधि बालिकुमार ॥६७क॥
निसिचर कीस लराई बरनिसि बिबिधि प्रकार ।
कुंभकरन घननाद कर बल पौरुष संघार ॥६७ख॥

चौपाई-caupāī:

निसिचर निकर मरन बिधि नाना । रघुपति रावन समर बखाना ॥
रावन बध मंदोदरि सोका । राज बिभीषन देव असोका ॥
सीता रघुपति मिलन बहोरी । सुरन्ह कीन्हि अस्तुति कर जोरी ॥
पुनि पुष्पक चढ़ि कपिन्ह समेता । अवध चले प्रभु कृपा निकेता ॥
जेहि बिधि राम नगर निज आए । बायस बिसद चरित सब गाए ॥
कहेसि बहोरि राम अभिषेका । पुर बरनत नृपनीति अनेका ॥
कथा समस्त भुसुंड बखानी । जो मैं तुम्ह सन कही भवानी ॥
सुनि सब राम कथा खगनाहा । कहत बचन मन परम उछाहा ॥

सोरठा-sorathā:

गयउ मोर संदेह सुनेउँ सकल रघुपति चरित ।
भयउ राम पद नेह तव प्रसाद बायस तिलक ॥६८क॥

-- इति श्रीमद्रामचरितमानसे सकलकलिकलुषविध्वंसने श्रीकाकभुसुंडिरामायण --

श्रीराघवं दशरथात्मजमप्रमेयं
सीतापतिं रघुकुलान्वयरत्नदीपम् ।
आजानुबाहुमरविन्ददलायताक्षं
रामं निशाचरविनाशकरं नमामि ॥

वैदेहीसहितं सुरद्रुमतले हैमे महामण्डपे
मध्ये पुष्पकमासने मणिमये वीरासने सुस्थितम् ।
अग्रे वाचयति प्रभञ्जनसुते तत्त्वं मुनिभ्यः परं
व्याख्यान्तं भरतादिभिः परिवृतं रामं भजे श्यामलम् ॥

श्रीरामो रामभद्रश्च रामचन्द्रश्च शाश्वतः ।
राजीवलोचनः श्रीमान् राजेन्द्रो रघुपुङ्गवः ॥ १ ॥

जानकीवल्लभो जैत्रो जितामित्रो जनार्दनः ।
विश्वामित्रप्रियो दान्तः शरणत्राणतत्परायः ॥ २ ॥

वालिप्रमथनो वाग्मी सत्यवाक् सत्यविक्रमः ।
सत्यव्रतो व्रतधरः सदा हनुमदाश्रितः ॥ ३ ॥

कौसलेयः खरध्वंसी विराधवधपण्डितः ।
विभीषणपरित्राता हरकोदण्डखण्डनः ॥ ४ ॥

सप्ततालप्रभेत्ता च दशग्रीवशिरोहरः ।
जामदग्न्यमहादर्पदलनस्ताटकान्तकः ॥ ५ ॥

वेदान्तसारो वेदात्मा भवरोगस्य भेषजम् ।
दूषणत्रिशिरो हन्ता त्रिमूर्तिस्त्रिगुणात्मकः ॥ ६ ॥

त्रिविक्रमस्त्रिलोकात्मा पुण्यचारित्रकीर्तनः ।
त्रिलोकरक्षको धन्वी दण्डकारण्यपावनः ॥ ७ ॥

अहल्याशापशमनः पितृभक्तो वरप्रदः ।
जितेन्द्रियो जितक्रोधो जितामित्रो जगद्गुरुः ॥ ८ ॥

ऋक्षवानरसंघाती चित्रकूटसमाश्रयः ।
जयन्तत्राणवरदः सुमित्रापुत्रसेवितः ॥ ९ ॥

सर्वदेवादिदेवश्च मृतवानरजीवनः ।
मायामारीचहन्ता च महादेवो महाभुजः ॥ १० ॥

सर्वदेवस्तुतः सौम्यो ब्रह्मण्यो मुनिसंस्तुतः ।
महायोगी महोदारः सुग्रीवेप्सितराज्यदः ॥ ११ ॥

सर्वपुण्याधिकफलः स्मृतसर्वाघनाशनः ।
आदिदेवो महादेवो महापूरुष एव च ॥ १२ ॥

पुण्योदयो दयासारः पुराणपुरुषोत्तमः ।
स्मितवक्त्रो मिताभाषी पूर्वभाषी च राघवः ॥ १३ ॥

अनन्तगुणगम्भीरो धीरोदात्तगुणोत्तमः ।
मायामानुषचारित्रो महादेवादिपूजितः ॥ १४ ॥

सेतुकृज्जितवारीशः सर्वतीर्थमयो हरिः ।
श्यामाङ्गः सुन्दरः शूरः पीतवासा धनुर्धरः ॥ १५ ॥

सर्वयज्ञाधिपो यज्वा जरामरणवर्जितः ।
शिवलिङ्गप्रतिष्ठाता सर्वावगुणवर्जितः ॥ १६ ॥

परमात्मा परं ब्रह्म सच्चिदानन्दविग्रहः ।
परं ज्योतिः परंधाम पराकाशः परात्परः ॥ १७ ॥

परेशः पारगः पारः सर्वदेवात्मकः परः ॥

॥ इति श्रीरामाष्टोत्तरशतनामस्तोत्रं सम्पूर्णम् ॥

ॐ श्रीरामाय नमः 1
ॐ रामभद्राय नमः 2
ॐ रामचन्द्राय नमः 3
ॐ शाश्वताय नमः 4
ॐ राजीवलोचनाय नमः 5
ॐ श्रीमते नमः 6
ॐ राजेन्द्राय नमः 7
ॐ रघुपुङ्गवाय नमः 8
ॐ जानकीवल्लभाय नमः 9
ॐ जैत्राय नमः 10
ॐ जितामित्राय नमः 11
ॐ जनार्दनाय नमः 12
ॐ विश्वामित्रप्रियाय नमः 13
ॐ दान्ताय नमः 14
ॐ शरणत्राणतत्पराय नमः 15
ॐ वालिप्रमथनाय नमः 16
ॐ वाग्मिने नमः 17
ॐ सत्यवाचे नमः 18
ॐ सत्यविक्रमाय नमः 19
ॐ सत्यव्रताय नमः 20
ॐ व्रतधराय नमः 21
ॐ सदाहनुमदाश्रिताय नमः 22
ॐ कौसलेयाय नमः 23
ॐ खरध्वंसिने नमः 24
ॐ विराधवधपंडिताय नमः 25
ॐ विभीषणपरित्रात्रे नमः 26
ॐ हरकोदण्डखण्डनाय नमः 27
ॐ सप्ततालप्रभेत्रे नमः 28
ॐ दशग्रीवशिरोहराय नमः 29
ॐ जामदग्न्यमहादर्पदलनाय नमः 30
ॐ ताटकान्तकाय नमः 31
ॐ वेदान्तसाराय नमः 32
ॐ वेदात्मने नमः 33
ॐ भवरोगस्य भेषजाय नमः 34
ॐ दूषणत्रिशिरोहन्त्रे नमः 35
ॐ त्रिमूर्तये नमः 36
ॐ त्रिगुणात्मकाय नमः 37
ॐ त्रिविक्रमाय नमः 38
ॐ त्रिलोकात्मने नमः 39
ॐ पुण्यचारित्रकीर्तनाय नमः 40
ॐ त्रिलोकरक्षकाय नमः 41
ॐ धन्विने नमः 42
ॐ दंडकारण्यवर्तनाय नमः 43
ॐ अहल्याशापविमोचनाय नमः 44
ॐ पितृभक्ताय नमः 45
ॐ वरप्रदाय नमः 46
ॐ जितेन्द्रियाय नमः 47
ॐ जितक्रोधाय नमः 48
ॐ जितमित्राय नमः 49
ॐ जगद्गुरवे नमः 50
ॐ ऋक्षवानरसङ्घातिने नमः 51
ॐ चित्रकूटसमाश्रयाय नमः 52

ॐ जयन्तत्राणवरदाय नमः 53
ॐ सुमित्रापुत्रसेविताय नमः 54
ॐ सर्वदेवादिदेवाय नमः 55
ॐ मृतवानरजीवनाय नमः 56
ॐ मायामारीचहन्त्रे नमः 57
ॐ महादेवाय नमः 58
ॐ महाभुजाय नमः 59
ॐ सर्वदेवस्तुताय नमः 60
ॐ सौम्याय नमः 61
ॐ ब्रह्मण्याय नमः 62
ॐ मुनिसंस्तुताय नमः 63
ॐ महायोगिने नमः 64
ॐ महोदराय नमः 65
ॐ सुग्रीवेप्सितराज्यदाय नमः 66
ॐ सर्वपुण्याधिकफलाय नमः 67
ॐ स्मृतसर्वौघनाशनाय नमः 68
ॐ आदिपुरुषाय नमः 69
ॐ परमपुरुषाय नमः 70
ॐ महापुरुषाय नमः 71
ॐ पुण्योदयाय नमः 72
ॐ दयासाराय नमः 73
ॐ पुराणपुरुषोत्तमाय नमः 74
ॐ स्मितवक्त्राय नमः 75
ॐ मितभाषिणे नमः 76
ॐ पूर्वभाषिणे नमः 77
ॐ राघवाय नमः 78
ॐ अनन्तगुणगम्भीराय नमः 79
ॐ धीरोदात्तगुणोत्तमाय नमः 80

ॐ मायामानुषचारित्राय नमः 81
ॐ महादेवादिपूजिताय नमः 82
ॐ सेतुकृते नमः 83
ॐ जितवाराशये नमः 84
ॐ सर्वतीर्थमयाय नमः 85
ॐ हरये नमः 86
ॐ श्यामाङ्गाय नमः 87
ॐ सुन्दराय नमः 88
ॐ शूराय नमः 89
ॐ पीतवाससे नमः 90
ॐ धनुर्धराय नमः 91
ॐ सर्वयज्ञाधिपाय नमः 92
ॐ यज्विने नमः 93
ॐ जरामरणवर्जिताय नमः 94
ॐ शिवलिङ्गप्रतिष्ठात्रे नमः 95
ॐ सर्वापगुणवर्जिताय नमः 96
ॐ परमात्मने नमः 97
ॐ परब्रह्मणे नमः 98
ॐ सच्चिदानन्दविग्रहाय नमः 99
ॐ परञ्ज्योतिषे नमः 100
ॐ परन्धाम्ने नमः 101
ॐ पराकाशाय नमः 102
ॐ परात्पराय नमः 103
ॐ परेशाय नमः 104
ॐ पारगाय नमः 105
ॐ पाराय नमः 106
ॐ सर्वदेवात्मकाय नमः 107
ॐ परस्मै नमः 108

भजे विशेषसुन्दरं समस्तपापखण्डनम् ।
स्वभक्तचित्तरञ्जनं सदैव राममद्वयम् ॥ १ ॥

जटाकलापशोभितं समस्तपापनाशकम् ।
स्वभक्तभीतिभङ्गनं भजे ह राममद्वयम् ॥ २ ॥

निजस्वरूपबोधकं कृपाकरं भवापहम् ।
समं शिवं निरञ्जनं भजे ह राममद्वयम् ॥ ३ ॥

सहप्रपञ्चकल्पितं ह्यनामरूपवास्तवम् ।
निराकृतिं निरामयं भजे ह राममद्वयम् ॥ ४ ॥

निष्प्रपञ्चनिर्विकल्पनिर्मलं निरामयम् ॥
चिदेकरूपसन्ततं भजे ह राममद्वयम् ॥ ५ ॥

भवाब्धिपोतरूपकं ह्यशेषदेहकल्पितम् ।
गुणाकरं कृपाकरं भजे ह राममद्वयम् ॥ ६ ॥

महावाक्यबोधकैर्विराजमनवाक्पदैः ।
परब्रह्म व्यापकं भजे ह राममद्वयम् ॥ ७ ॥

शिवप्रदं सुखप्रदं भवच्छिदं भ्रमापहम् ।
विराजमानदैशिकं भजे ह राममद्वयम् ॥ ८ ॥

रामाष्टकं पठति यः सुकरं सुपुण्यं व्यासेन भाषितमिदं शृणुते मनुष्यः ।
विद्यां श्रियं विपुलसौख्यमनन्तकीर्तिं सम्प्राप्य देहविलये लभते च मोक्षम् ॥ ९ ॥

॥ इति श्रीव्यासविरचितं रामाष्टकं सम्पूर्णम् ॥

श्रीनामरामायणम - śrī nāma rāmāyaṇam

-- बालकाण्डः -- bālakāṇḍaḥ --

शुद्धब्रह्मपरात्पर राम .1.

कालात्मकपरमेश्वर राम .2.

शेषतल्पसुखनिद्रित राम .3.

ब्रह्माद्यमरप्रार्थित राम .4.

चण्डकिरणकुलमण्डन राम .5.

श्रीमद्दशरथनन्दन राम .6.

कौसल्यासुखवर्धन राम .7.

विश्वामित्रप्रियधन राम .8.

घोरताटकाघातक राम .9.

मारीचादिनिपातक राम .10.

कौशिकमखसंरक्षक राम .11.

श्रीमदहल्योद्धारक राम .12.

गौतममुनिसम्पूजित राम .13.

सुरमुनिवरगणसंस्तुत राम .14

नाविकधाविकमृदुपद राम .15.

मिथिलापुरजनमोहक राम .16.

विदेहमानसरञ्जक राम .17.

त्र्यंबककार्मुखभञ्जक राम .18.

सीतार्पितवरमालिक राम .19.

कृतवैवाहिककौतुक राम .20.

भार्गवदर्पविनाशक राम .21.

श्रीमदयोध्यापालक राम .22.

राम राम जय राजा राम - राम राम जय सीता राम

-- अयोध्याकाण्डः -- ayodhyākāṇḍaḥ --

अगणितगुणगणभूषित राम .23.

अवनीतनयाकामित राम .24.

राकाचन्द्रसमानन राम .25.

पितृवाक्याश्रितकानन राम .26.

प्रियगुहविनिवेदितपद राम .27.

तत्क्षालितनिजमृदुपद राम .28.

भरद्वाजमुखानन्दक राम .29.

चित्रकूटाद्रिनिकेतन राम .30.

दशरथसन्ततचिन्तित राम .31.

कैकेयीतनयार्पित राम .32.

विरचितनिजपितृकर्मक राम .33.

भरतार्पितनिजपादुक राम .34.

राम राम जय राजा राम - राम राम जय सीता राम

-- अरण्यकाण्डः -- araṇyakāṇḍaḥ --

दण्डकावनजनपावन राम .35.

दुष्टविराधविनाशन राम .36.

शरभङ्गसुतीक्ष्णार्चित राम .37.

अगस्त्यानुग्रहवर्दित राम .38.

गृध्राधिपसंसेवित राम .39.

पञ्चवटीतटसुस्थित राम .40.

शूर्पणखार्त्तिविधायक राम ..41.

खरदूषणमुखसूदक राम .42.

सीताप्रियहरिणानुग राम .43.

मारीचार्तिकृताशुग राम .44.

विनष्टसीतान्वेषक राम .45.

गृध्राधिपगतिदायक राम .46.

शबरीदत्तफलाशन राम .47.

कबन्धबाहुच्छेदन राम .48.

राम राम जय राजा राम - राम राम जय सीता राम

-- किष्किन्धाकाण्डः -- kiṣkindhākāṇḍaḥ --

हनुमत्सेवितनिजपद राम rāma .49.

नतसुग्रीवाभीष्टद राम .50.

गर्वितवालिसंहारक राम .51.

वानरदूतप्रेषक राम .52.

हितकरलक्ष्मणसंयुत राम .53.

राम राम जय राजा राम - राम राम जय सीता राम

-- सुन्दरकाण्डः -- sundarakāṇḍaḥ --

कपिवरसन्ततसंस्मृत राम .54.

तद्गतिविघ्नध्वंसक राम .55.

सीताप्राणाधारक राम .56.

दुष्टदशाननदूषित राम .57.

शिष्टहनूमद्भूषित राम .58.

सीतवेदितकाकावन राम .59.

कृतचूडामणिदर्शन राम .60.

कपिवरवचनाश्वासित राम .61.

राम राम जय राजा राम - राम राम जय सीता राम

-- युद्धकाण्डः -- yuddhakāṇḍaḥ --

रावणनिधनप्रस्थित राम .62.

वानरसैन्यसमावृत राम .63.

शोषितशरदीशार्त्तित राम .64.

विभीष्णाभयदायक राम .65.

पर्वतसेतुनिबन्धक राम .66.

कुम्भकर्णशिरश्छेदन राम .67.

राक्षससङ्घविमर्धक राम .68.

अहिमहिरावणचारण राम .69.

संहृतदशमुखरावण राम .70.

विधिभवमुखसुरसंस्तुत राम .71

खःस्थितदशरथवीक्षित राम .72.

सीतादर्शनमोदित राम .73.

अभिषिक्तविभीषणनुत राम .74.

पुष्पकयानारोहण राम .75.

भरद्वाजादिनिषेवण राम .76.

भरतप्राणप्रियकर राम .77.

साकेतपुरीभूषण राम .78.

सकलस्वीयसमानस राम .79.

रत्नलसत्पीठास्थित राम .80.

पट्टाभिषेकालंकृत राम .81.

पार्थिवकुलसम्मानित राम .82.

विभीषणार्पितरङ्गक राम .83.

कीशकुलानुग्रहकर राम .84.

सकलजीवसंरक्षक राम .85.

समस्तलोकोद्धारक राम .86.

राम राम जय राजा राम - राम राम जय सीता राम

-- उत्तरकाण्डः -- uttarakāṇḍaḥ --

आगत मुनिगण संस्तुत राम .87.

विश्रुतदशकण्ठोद्भव राम .88.

सितालिङ्गननिर्वृत राम .89.

नीतिसुरक्षितजनपद राम .90.

विपिनत्याजितजनकज राम .91.

कारितलवणासुरवध राम .92.

स्वर्गतचम्बुक संस्तुत राम .93.

स्वतनयकुशलवनन्दित राम .94.

अश्वमेधक्रतुदिक्षित राम .95.

कालावेदितसुरपद राम .96.

आयोध्यकजनमुक्तित राम .97.

विधिमुखविभुदानन्दक राम .98.

तेजोमयनिजरूपक राम .99.

संसृतिबन्धविमोचक राम .100.

धर्मस्थापनतत्पर राम .101.

भक्तिपरायणमुक्तिद राम .102.

सर्वचराचरपालक राम .103.

सर्वभवामयवारक राम .104.

वैकुण्ठालयसंस्तित राम .105.

नित्यनन्दपदस्तित राम .106.

राम राम जय राजा राम .107.

राम राम जय सीता राम .108.

राम राम जय राजा राम - राम राम जय सीता राम

राम राम जय राजा राम - राम राम जय सीता राम

श्री राम-स्तुति — śrī rāma-stuti

श्री रामचन्द्र कृपालु भजु मन हरण भवभय दारुणं,
नवकंज-लोचन कंज-मुख कर-कंज पद कंजारुणं. 1
कंदर्प अगणित अमित छवि नवनील नीरद सुंदरं,
पट पीत मानहु तड़ित रुचि शुचि नौमि जनक सुतावरं. 2
भजु दीनबंधु दिनेश दानव-दैत्य-वंश निकंदनं,
रघुनंद आनँदकंद कोशलचंद दशरथ नंदनं. 3
सिर मुकुट कुंडल तिलक चारु उदारु अंग विभूषणं,
आजानुभुज शर-चाप-धर संग्राम-जित-खरदूषणं. 4
इति वदति तुलसीदास शंकर-शेष-मुनि-मन-रंजनं,
मम हृदय कंज निवास करु कामादि खल-दल-गंजनं. 5
श्री रामचन्द्र कृपालु भजु मन हरण भवभय दारुणं ...

::

श्री हनुमान-स्तुति — śrī hanumāna-stuti

मंगल-मूरति मारुत-नंदन , सकल-अमंगल-मूल-निकंदन. 1
पवन-तनय संतन-हितकारी , हृदय विराजत अवध बिहारी. 2
मातु-पिता गुरु गनपति सारद , सिवा-समेत संभु सुक-नारद. 3
चरन बंदि बिनवौं सब काहू , देहु रामपद-नेह-निबाहू. 4
बंदौं राम-लखन-बैदेही , जे तुलसी के परम सनेही. 5
मंगल-मूरति मारुत-नंदन ...

—o—

सियावर रामचन्द्र की जय
siyāvara rāmacandra kī jaya
पवनसुत हनुमान की जय
pavanasuta hanumāna kī jaya
गोस्वामी तुलसीदास की जय
gosvāmī tulasīdāsa kī jaya

—o—

Thank you and congratulations on possessing this splendid book on the glories of our Lord. Help us to reach out to more people. Please consider telling your friends about these Holy-Hymns—or gift them a copy. Do please leave your ratings/reviews on Amazon and elsewhere to help spread the word. Thank you.

Jaya Hanumān. Jaya Sītā-Rāma.

सीताराम सीताराम सीताराम राम राम, रामराम रामराम रामराम सीता राम
sītārāma sītārāma sītārāma rāma rāma, rāmarāma rāmarāma rāmarāma sītā rāma

Guide to Pronunciation

The following points will prove useful in learning to pronounce Devnāgrī words.

VOWELS

Trans-literation	Devnāgrī Vowel in Standalone-Form	Description	Devnāgrī vowel in Mātrā-Form (examples shown with consonant स)
a	अ	Vowel, short 'a', sounds like the **u** in s**u**m	स
ā	आ	Vowel, long 'a', sounds like the **a** in saga	सा
i	इ	Vowel, short 'i', sounds like the **i** in s**i**t	सि
ī	ई	Vowel, long 'i', sounds like the **ee** in s**ee**k	सी
u	उ	Vowel, short 'u', sounds like the **u** in s**u**per	सु
ū	ऊ	Vowel, long 'u', sounds like the **oo** in s**oo**t	सू
e	ए	Vowel, short 'ai', sounds like the **ay** in s**ay**	से
ai	ऐ	Vowel, long 'ai', sounds like the **a** in sag	सै
o	ओ	Vowel, short 'o', sounds like the **o** in s**o**ul	सो
au	औ	Vowel, long 'o', sounds like the **aw** in s**aw**	सौ

- Vowels are written in Standalone form, or in Mātrā form with a consonant. Listed above are the 5 main vowels, in their short & long tones. More vowels exist.
- Short vowels (**a, i, u, e, o**) are pronounced a certain way and their long equivalents (**ā, ī, ū, ai, au**) receive additional stress on those short sounds.
- ऋ (ṛ) is another vowel. In Mātrā form it is written as the curve below some constant; e.g. कृ - kṛ ('crunch').
- **ṃ ṁ m̐** are modifiers which have the effect of nasalizing the preceding sound.
- **ḥ** is a vowel modifier: a rough breathing that causes the preceding vowel to echo.

CONSONANTS

For the most part Consonants sound just as in English; but do please be cognizant of the following:

- Devnāgrī Consonants are mostly pronounced with the inherent sound of short **a** at the end*, unless another vowel modifies that sound. e.g. consider म-ma ('**mu**st') versus the vowel modified म-m like: मा-mā ('**mar**k'), मि-mi ('**mi**ss'), मी-mī ('**mee**k'), मु-mu ('**mu**dra'), मू-mū ('**moo**n') , मे-me ('**may**') , मै-mai ('**ma**n') , मो-mo ('**mo**re') , मौ-mau ('**mau**l'), मं-maṁ ('**mum**').

*Exception: A Devnāgrī consonant in its pristine form (e.g. म् [in rare use and] which has a diacritic mark) or a half form (e.g. सम्मान) will not have the sound of short vowel 'a' at end.

- **c** is always pronounced like the **ch** in **ch**uck. [so then expect words like clear written as **k**lear]
- **ch** may also be approximated to **c** but with added aspiration like in the sneezing sound.
- **d** is soft like in **th**us.
- **ḍ** is hard like in **d**ust.
- **g** is hard like in **g**ranite.
- **ṅ** sounds approx. like the **ng** in hu**ng**.
- **ñ** is the ny sounds like the **ni** in on**i**on.
- **s** without the diacritic is like the normal **s**, as in **s**um.
- **ś** and **ṣ** have very subtle difference that may be ignored, and can be approximated to the **sh** in **sh**ut.
- **ṭ** is hard like in **t**ough.
- **t** is soft. Difficult to approximate but try saying **t**hird without the h.
- Unlike English, Devnāgrī distinguishes between un-aspirated consonant and aspirated consonants (with a succeeding **h**). So we have **bh, ch, dh, ḍh, gh, jh, kh, ph, th, ṭh** etc.

Some of Our Other Books for You

- **Tulsi Ramayana--The Hindu Bible**: Ramcharitmanas with English Translation & Transliteration
  8.5" x 11" ISBN: 978-1-945739-01-9 (Paperback) ISBN: 978-1-945739-03-3 (Hardcover)
- **Ramcharitmanas**: Ramayana of Tulsidas with Transliteration
  8.5" x 11" ISBN: 978-1-945739-00-2 (Paperback) ISBN: 978-1-945739-02-6 (Hardcover)

TULSI RAMAYANA-THE HINDU BIBLE
Original Text + Translation + Transliteration
8.5" x 11".
Font shown is actual size (approx.)
धन्य देस सो जहँ सुरसरी । धन्य नारि पतिब्रत अनुसरी ॥
dhanya desa so jahaṁ surasarī, dhanya nāri patibrata anusarī.
धन्य सो भूपु नीति जो करई । धन्य सो द्विज निज धर्म न टरई ॥
dhanya so bhūpu nīti jo karaī, dhanya so dvija nija dharma na ṭaraī.
सो धन धन्य प्रथम गति जाकी । धन्य पुन्य रत मति सोइ पाकी ॥
so dhana dhanya prathama gati jākī, dhanya punya rata mati soi pākī.
बिनु हरि कृपा न होइ सो गावहिं बेद पुरान ॥ १२५ख॥
binu hari kṛpā na hoi so gāvahiṁ beda purāna. 125(kha).
After affectionately bowing his head at his feet, Garud proceeded to Vaikunth, with Rāma's image impressed upon his heart. O Girijā, there is no blessing like that of communion with the saints; it is attainable only by Hari's grace so the Vedas and Purāns declare.
RAM-CHARIT-MANAS
Original Text + Transliteration
8.5" x 11".
Font shown is actual size (approx.)
सुंदर मनोहर मंदिरायत अजिर रुचिर फटिक रचे ।
suṁdara manohara maṁdirāyata ajira rucira phaṭika race,
प्रति द्वार द्वार कपाट पुरट बनाइ बहु बज्रन्हि खचे ॥
prati dvāra dvāra kapāṭa puraṭa banāī bahu bajranhi khace.
चारु चित्रसाला गृह गृह प्रति लिखे बनाइ ।
cāru citrasālā gṛha gṛha prati likhe banāī,
ग्यान गिरा गोतीत अज माया मन गुन पार ।
gyāna girā gotīta aja māyā mana guna pāra,
सोइ सच्चिदानंद घन कर नर चरित उदार ॥ २५॥
soi saccidānaṁda ghana kara nara carita udāra. 25.
प्रातकाल सरऊ करि मज्जन । बैठहिं सभाँ संग द्विज सज्जन ॥
prātakāla saraū kari majjana, baiṭhahiṁ sabhāṁ saṁga dvija sajjana.

Some of Our Other Books for You

- **Ramayana, Large**: Tulsi Ramcharitmanas, Hindi only Edition
  8.5" x 11" ISBN: 978-1-945739-06-4 (Paperback) ISBN: 978-1-945739-10-1 (Hardcover)
- **Ramayana, Medium**: Tulsi Ramcharitmanas, Hindi only Edition
  8" x 10" ISBN: 978-1-945739-12-5 (Paperback) ISBN: 978-1-945739-11-8 (Hardcover)

ABOUT RĀMCHARITMĀNAS AND TULSĪDĀS

Cheerfully and lovingly recited by all the devotees of Bhagwān Rāma, Rāmcharitmānas, the Epic-of-Rāma, is a veritable fount of Devotion and Wisdom known to dispel away evil and ignorance. Established through all the dominions of earth, this timeless saga of the ancient most Being Rāma has been narrated by many a great Rishīs of past; and once again to trumpet it in the Kali-Yuga, the holy story of Rāma, Lord of Hanumān, has been penned by the wonderful saint Tulsīdās—from a quill fashioned with the very feathers of a Param-Haṁsa, the divine bird of highest discrimination and wisdom—and written dipped in the sweetness of Nectar of Devotion.

Tulsīdās, born in India in the sixteenth century, was an illustrious saint, philosopher, poet, and a supreme devotee of Bhagwān Rāma, the incarnate Supreme Being. He composed many poems in praise of Shrī Rāma, with Rāmcharitmānas being his most celebrated epic. Though he was an eminent Sanskrit scholar he chose to write in Awadhī, the language of the populace, so that all could sing the glories of Lord God Rāma.

The potency and beauty of Tulsīdās' poetry is unparalleled in the history of literature. Rāmcharitmānas, intended as the religious instruction for all—literate or illiterate, even those who have absolutely no knowledge of the Vedas—is the quintessence of Sanātana-Dharma; and the verses of Rāmcharitmānas may be compared to Mantras: containing the gist of the highest truths culled from the Vedas and Purānas.

By churning the wealth that is contained in many religious works and in many discourses based on Dharma, the nectar of Rāmcharitmānas—comprising of the highest knowledge and most sublime devotion—has been raised by Rishī Tulsīdās. As ghee is created from milk for the benefit of a beloved, even so has Rāmcharitmānas been churned out by Tulsīdās for the sake of Rāma Devotees—simply out of compassion and love that only a parent can have for their child. Our repeated obeisance to the parent of every Devotee: Bhakta Shiromanī Param Rāma Bhakta Sant Rishī Tulsīdās Jī.

The Vedas and Purānas are oceans of wisdom; and when the intellect of a seer like Tulsīdās shines upon them, then, seared from its fieriness, some of that sapience evaporates; and further, when those cumulous clouds of profundity condense under the cooling influence of compassion of that saint's lovesome heart, then they pour in as snow upon the sublime heights of Himalayas called the Rāmcharitmānas; and then from those lofty heights, multiple streams of the wonderful confluence of Wisdom and Devotion are seen forevermore in a relentless flow: as the Ganges of Rāma-Kathā, for the thirsting humanity.

Within Rāmcharitmānas, Tulsīdās has caught the essence of the mystic susurrations of Vedic chants; and their ancient rhythm has become woven into a simple rustic poetry in his artful words and deft hands. Verily the bright searing heat from the sun of Vedic wisdom is seen congealed into the cooling beams of full-moon light in Tulsīdās' verses sublime—which bring restful solace to one and all who have read them just but once. And these verses of Rāmcharitmānas—when sung or heard, whether understood or not—when their charming beauty has inundated you with bliss, and when their sound floats away driven by the dictates of the laws of nature—then they do not mingle far but remain suspended in space, clinging around you, and they wrap you in an aura of hushed serenity which carries you on a cloud of calm, through the intensity of entire day.

(*Above culled from books in the:* **Upanishad Vidya (Know Thyself) Series.** *Authored by:* **Vidya Wati**)

(8.5" x 11" x 450 pages ISBN: 978-1-945739-01-9 (Paperback) ISBN: 978-1-945739-03-3 (Hardcover)

Rāmcharitmānas, the scripture studied religiously by millions of Hindus across the world everyday, is a most Holy Writ: blessed, divine, sublime. It is a sanctified scripture rife with its own wonderful intrinsic power that sanctifies; and it is renowned to cure the maladies of body, mind, soul, life. As if possessing some magical attributes, there is something which makes Rāmcharitmānas so charming and profound—but that something has not been discovered even until now.

Of course being the Epic of Lord God Rāma, the appeal, enchantment, and profoundness replete herein, should lend itself to no wonderment; but then again, the charm also results because these divine verses come to us through the medium of a remarkable seer and saint, a supreme devotee of Lord Rāma, a true man of God, an empyreal bard: Sant Tulsīdās.

As you study this holy scripture—also known as the Tulsī Rāmāyana—let it be known: The real substance of this book is the original verses of Tulsīdās. Remove them from the book—or ignore them during the reading—and less than one percent of the book will remain; And that is the reason why we have rendered the original Tulsī text into Transliterated form as well: so that the benefits of reading the Tulsī Rāmāyana can be earned in full by one and all.

And although we also give English portrayal of the verses to suggest to the reader what is going on but we consider these to be simply merely hints, and deem them as having little import beyond that. The so-called 'Translation' is not the real deal, if you will, but just a shadowy clue—which is the best that one can do. Yes; to present the work of a literary giant like Tulsīdās, through the medium of Translation, is a most daunting task and we will not even begin to attempt that. We prefer to call this venture not a Translation but simply a decrepit depiction in English words of the Tulsī Rāmāyana.

In the past, numerous great souls have rendered the Rāmcharitmānas into Hindi, English, and various other languages, and we are greatly indebted to all of them—for we have copiously made use of the several existing works to cumulate this work here. All the credit goes only to such noble souls who have written and discoursed upon this great Epic over the years, and only the mistakes originate from me: a little bee floundering, who flew to many beautiful flowers, but being incapable, could not gather the nectar well enough.

Now, without further ado, most humbly, sitting at his blessed feet, this book is placed in the hands of our family deity Shrī Hanumān, the most favorite attendant of Shrī Rāma, and may he do what he pleases with it.

(**Baldev Prasad Saxena** -- Compiler-Translator-Editor of: Tulsi Ramayana--The Hindu Bible)

(6.1" x 9.2" x 108 pages ISBN: 978-1-945739-05-7 (Paperback)

Such souls are truly blessed: who drink of the nectar which is the name 'Rāma'—which nectar has been churned out of the all-pervading ocean of Brahmn—which nectar may be availed of as much as desired but never becomes depleted—which nectar remains ever present on the moon-like beautiful face of Lord Shankar increasing his beauty—which nectar is the sole remedy for all worldly afflictions—which nectar is the provider of all bliss—which nectar is the very life of mother Jānakī Sītā.

Blessed is our Lord God Sītā-Rāma and blessed the devotees of Sītā-Rāma: who remain ever absorbed in the joy of devotion to their Lord; who have thrown their heart as fish into the nectarine lake of love for the beautiful name Sītā-Rāma—two redeeming words, easy to remember, most delightful to hear, utter, sing; which satisfy every wish, and are the highest gain in this world and the next.

Blessed are such noble souls, who have heard the word, and who now understand, and who find themselves almost there; or who, in the spirit of devotion, have taken their first plunge; but the blessed-most are those who have already attained eternal happiness in the sea of serenity called Sītā-Rāma. But what about the rest of us? How will I secure my own release from this endless cycle of transmigration? Having Bhakti and submission to our Lord is the surest means of gaining deliverance from the cruel cycle of births and deaths—easy to say, but how do we attain to that? How far is it from here to there? And how do we get there? Who will be gracious to me? Who will inspire me with devotion to the lotus feet of Sītā-Rāma? In these difficult times, how is one to inculcate Devotion to the Lord's feet, and furthermore sustain it?

The answer is Tulsīdās' Rāmacaritamānas.

Yes, Rāmacaritamānas, the divine song—which emerged from the beautiful Mānas Lake of Lord Shiva's soul—which is the celestial river replete with Rāma's bright renown that has been in a relentless flow for eons—in whose holy torrents are swept away all the impurities of the Kali-Yug, whether they be in the form of tiny blades of grass or mighty trees tall—in the proximity of which you find your soul in an overflowing swell of ecstatic devotion—and submerged in whose streams you find your heart welling with joy and rapture.

Verily Rāmacaritamānas imparts Bhakti—as millions over the ages have discovered and aver. Its recitation helps us inculcate the habit of constantly remembering Bhagwān Rāma: to focus our minds upon Him, and His Holy Name. This is the supreme easy path of Hinduism known as Bhakti-Yog—finding God through Devotion. Bhakti for Sītā-Rāma, Hanumān, is the infallible remedy for all worldly ills and misfortunes which you see spreading like wildfire in this Kali-Yug.

Not just imparting the highest bliss of emancipation, Rāmacaritamānas delivers at every level—be it worldly or spiritual. After a hard day's toil, one finds a fount of rejuvenation within the verses of Tulsīdās; and just as a fish feels fresh when submerged in water, so too our souls feel invigorated by taking a dip in the Ocean of Bliss called Rāma—which Ocean exists within Rāmacaritamānas: the holy water of divine enactments and stories of Lord Rāma—which deeds were recorded by Lord Shiva Himself; and which have percolated down to us through several different narrators—with Goswāmī Tulsīdās being the latest in the long chain. Tulsīdās recorded the Rāmacaritamānas in his rustic poetry and his books are like pitchers full of ambrosia for gaining everlasting peace within our soul.

With the blessings of Lord Shiva, the verses of Rāmacaritamānas have acquired the power of Mantras. Each verse within Rāmacaritamānas is like a Siddha-Mantra—this the multitudes have testified over the centuries. Not only does Rāmacaritamānas bring the Supreme Being nearer to our hearts than ever before—making spiritual liberation and deliverance easily available—but the worldly benefits she brings to us are endless too. As myriads of devotees have verified through experiences of direct grace, Rāmacaritamānas, the Epic of Rāma, is like a Kāmadhenu—the celestial cow—which yields whatever the devotee seeks from her, be it some worldly remedy or spiritual enlightenment.

Amongst the people, Sundarakāṇḍa, the fifth ascent into Rāmacaritamānas has become the most popular Canto of the great Epic. Often it is often sung independently and is considered a book in itself. It is called Sundara because it is Beautiful, and it is Beautiful for its various reasons; especially since the sorrowful events of Ayodhyā-Kānd, this episode rekindles hope.

The Fifth Canto of Rāmacaritamānas bridges many ends and in it one finds many wishes being granted—which span the spectrum of human desires. In the same vein, numerous Rāma devotees over the centuries have averred, after direct realization, that the Pāṭha (recitation) of Rāmacaritamānas (or her proxy, the Sundarakāṇḍa) has the power to grant you any wish which you harbor in your heart; and during their recitation, they use the Samputṣ of certain verses taken from within the Rāmacaritamānas to get their desired wish.

Samputṭ or Samputṭikaran is a Mantra which adds potency to the verses being hymned; in essence, it is a Mantra within a Mantra. Considered very powerful, Samputṭ Mantras are mostly Chaupaīs or Dohās from within the Rāmacaritamānas itself; or they are the various chants of 'Rāma'—the King of Holy Mantras.

There are many Mantras in Rāmacaritamānas which are used to ward off troubles and afflictions as well as to gain the favor of our Lord God. For instance many parents will do the Pāṭha of Sundarakāṇḍa on the birthday of their children or loved ones using the following Mantra:

अजर अमर गुननिधि सुत होहू । करहुँ बहुत रघुनायक छोहू ॥
ajara amara gunanidhi suta hohū, karahuṁ bahuta raghunāyaka chohū.

which means: **May you, dear, become ageless, deathless and a treasury of virtues and the very beloved of Shrī Rāma.** This is the boon which mother Sītā bestows upon Hanumān in verse 5.17.3 of Rāmacaritamānas (the 3rd Chaupaī leading up to Dohā 17 of the Fifth Canto, Sundarakāṇḍa).

Similarly, to gain the favor of Lord God and for the welfare and general well-being of their family, people will add the following Samputṭ Mantra during their weekly Sundarakāṇḍa Pātha:

मंगल भवन अमंगल हारी । द्रवउ सो दसरथ अजिर बिहारी ॥
maṁgala bhavana amaṁgala hārī, dravau so dasaratha ajira bihārī.

meaning: **He, who is the bane of all woes and an Abode of Bliss, who sports in the courtyards of King Dasrath, may that compassionate child Rāma, be ever kind to me.** This verse is spoken by Lord Shiva to Uma at Rāmacaritamānas 1.112.4.

(**Subhash Chandra** -- Author of **Sundarakanda -- The Fifth-Ascent of Tulsi Ramayana**)

The Upanishad Vidya Series

Vedas, the ancient most human compositions, end in Vedanta: the "Culmination-of-Vedas". Vedanta—containing the philosophical parts of Vedas—comprises of many Upanishads. Our Upanishad Vidya series gives the 'Gist of Upanishads' in an easy to understand language.

RAMA GOD: In The Beginning - Upanishad Vidya (Know Thyself) Author: Vidya Wati.
ISBN: **9781945739217** (Paperback), **9781945739224** (Hardback)

Eastern wisdom—a continual meditation on Life, Death, Self, Immortality—has inspired and puzzled wisdom seekers for ages. Expressing these philosophical, spiritual ideas in poetic words that are simultaneously lucid, and insightful, this book reveals the ultimate reality—taking one on a journey beyond death: to the portals of eternal life. The theme of Vedanta is presented here in an easy to understand language through the lips of Tulsidas, a sixteenth century saint, who is on his travels in a fictional journey through parts of India. This book is the "First Gem" in the continuing "Upanishad Vidya" Series. Here we can hear the audacious voice of the saint go rolling through the multitudes:

"I am. I am the Self—the Self whose essence is the snow-white flux of consciousness. My real nature is pureness without a hint of blemishes. Minus a beginning, minus an end, I am the dominion that ever am; and I am the light that can never be snuffed-out, extinguished. I am the element coalesced from the flux of luminance; and I am the Sun, and the child of Sun—emerged from the womb of endless space. A light-beam torn from the stars, I am the soul upon its circular journey—to the ocean of radiance. Of Rāma, within Rāma—I am the child of blessedness.

Where am I? Where the head is void and quiet the heart reposed; where the world...like a hollow murmur rings; where mute forever abides the voice,—the one that's there, who's still in here: that one is me; O yes, that one's me. *Who am I?* Where joys and sorrows turn back, return ...away; from where every single thought ... ...runs away; that singularity of awareness, the purity of simply being: that one is me; ...yes, that is me.

Motionless below an abeyant arch; where is no sunlight above, and neath, no shadows curve; where no waves of dualities ever swing; the one there alone, who ever sings, —that one is me, ... is me."

Yes—not the cacophonous sounds of shuddering despair and doom; or the grating noise from chains that generations dragged across dark thresholds through chapels of gloom; or the babbling words of hell, satan, sin, and damnation; or a rumpus of the falling ruins rising from the depths of unavailing bleak faith—this was the voice of the Free, the proclamation of the Fearless, the sound that sets one Free.

Purling Shadows: And a Dream called Life - Upanishad Vidya (Know Thyself) Author: Vidya Wati.
ISBN: **9781945739231** (Paperback), **9781945739248** (Hardback)

This life is but a dream! In an unbridled setting for fascinating tales spun out by someone wacky and wild, or perhaps like a playful child, and with one huge blue canvas before him and a palette of monstrous colors to the side, this life is but infinite painted dreams—dreams that transcend the ambit of all sane possibilities.

In a vast land of imagery—so beautiful and such carefully wrought—stroking a wonderful complexity of its infinite threads; sinking his finger into them but without truly feeling their touch; with many imagined knots rolled tightly into a ball—but held in a loose clasp; dreaming on and on with his wide lustrous open eyes—languid and yet bright; gazing at an undulating canvas covering the whole of the wall; creating and working to make many things come alive, just so that he can eventually commemorate their deaths—there is this One Insane Being—of incomprehensible merit and wondrous brilliance—and of such an aching consciousness, and a mind full of wistful play. Him—God—who can ever really fully understand?

And when fatigued of some play then, with one soft cold touch of his thought, he just pushes things all aside, making them simply mute, blending them quietly away—a fade out as some would say.

And lies here this pitiful heap, gathered of his broken bits; and he takes a moment to stop and gaze at it; then idly he rearranges it all into a beautiful new artifact—caring not even to add his name upon it, before or after. “To be known, and to propel your name into futurity it’s a requisite to write your name upon it”—I shout out to him, but he cares not the least. A Majestic Madman of such divine qualities indeed—now him, who can ever truly understand?

And O, how can I even begin to tell you what I see in his eyes! And at times I too become one with his unhinged cerebrations of the crazed kind—where all things are found simply to shine—even those things that are the most unkind; and where no sighs drift up to us from the woes of the earth below; and where no griefs ever touch us while we are with him there.

(Book names may slightly change at time of Release)

Lost Soul - Upanishad Vidya (Know Thyself)	Author: Vidya Wati	Release date: Fall 2018
The Orb - Upanishad Vidya (Know Thyself)	Author: Vidya Wati	Release date: Winter 2018
Fiery Circle - Upanishad Vidya (Know Thyself)	Author: Vidya Wati	Release date: 2019

Sundarakāṇḍa
सुन्दरकाण्ड
Ramcharitmanas
रामचरितमानस
PURLING
Shadows
UPANISHAD VIDYA
KNOW
THYSELF
FOOL
Rāma-Hymns
राम-जप
TULSI
rāmayana
THE HINDU BIBLE
रामचरितमानस
FIRST
KNOW
THYSELF
O
FOOL
RAMA
God
Vidya Wati
रामचरितमानस
रामचरितमानस

www.ingramcontent.com/pod-product-compliance
Lightning Source LLC
Chambersburg PA
CBHW021444080526
44588CB00009B/686
* 9 7 8 1 9 4 5 7 3 9 2 5 5 *